CARRIED ON THE WIND

First published in 2003 by
WOODFIELD PUBLISHING
Bognor Regis, West Sussex, England
www.woodfieldpublishing.com

ISBN 1-903953-45-6

Carried on the Wind

*Wartime Experiences of a Special Duties Operator
with No.101 Squadron RAF Bomber Command*

SEAN FEAST

Woodfield

Flt/Lt Ted Manners with Vesuvius in background.

CONTENTS

Nose art on Avro Lancaster LL757 – W – Oor Wullie

Introduction

Three years ago I wanted to write a book about the life of my Great Uncle Peter, a bomb aimer in 150 Squadron shot down and killed in December 1944 on his 22nd Op. It would be a present for my mother for the Millennium about a man she never really knew, as she was only five at the time he was reported missing.

My father suggested I spoke to his former boss, a man he had worked with at the London and Lancashire Insurance Company (which ultimately became The Royal Insurance) who he knew had been in the RAF, in Lancasters. That man was Ted Manners.

Ted, I hope he won't mind me for saying, doesn't say very much, but what he does say is usually worth listening to. When I met with him and his lovely wife Annie and abused their hospitality appallingly, not only was he very helpful in providing me with an insight into the life of a typical Bomber Command crew, but it also became clear that his story, and that of his squadron, would be one I would like to research.

Through Ted I was able to meet or correspond with the six other surviving crew members – Rusty, Alec, Curly, Norman, Taffy and Harry – and all were unstinting in their help and support, and I think pleased – if that is the word – that a comparative youngster (me!) had taken such an interest in some dear old buffers in the twilight of their years!

The result, is this story. A remarkable story. And all of it is true.

About the Author

Sean Feast started his career in journalism and PR. Now a Director of The AGA Group, the UK's leading independent business-to-business communications agency, he is still a regular contributor to a number of newspapers and business magazines. Married to Elaine and with two small boys, he lives in Hertfordshire. *Carried on the Wind* is his second book.

Prologue

They were less than 40 miles from the target, the railway marshalling yards at Hasselt in Belgium, when it happened. Suddenly, Curly, the Flight Engineer, let out a cry of alarm over the intercom: "Bloody hell skip – look out!". Tommy, the mid-upper, had seen it too. But they were the only ones, and by then it was already too late.

Through the gloom and broken cloud, the huge but unmistakable shape of another four-engined bomber appeared from below on the starboard quarter. It was a terrifying sight. They had braved searchlights, flak and nightfighters over arguably the most fiercely defended City in Germany at the height of the Battle of Berlin. They had come through unscathed the Bloody Massacres that were Nuremberg and Mailly-Le-Camp when they had lost almost half the squadron. And they were now only a handful of trips from completing their tour over the relatively 'safe' invasion targets of Northern France.

But this was something none of them could have anticipated. The end. A mid-air collision. Not a glorious death, if death could ever be so. Instead, brought down by one of their own aircraft. And there was nothing they could do. No-one called for evasive action, but by then it was too late anyway. As it was, it probably saved their lives.

Before Curly had finished his expletives the two aircraft had already collided, the unidentified Lancaster's mid-upper turret and propeller blades ripping through *A Wing and a Prayer* fuselage and bomb bay, tearing its secret ABC aerial from its body, and seriously damaging the tailplane and bottom of its inboard engine nacelles.

Harry, the rear gunner, heard Curly's shout and sensed the aircraft shudder and seem to stop in mid-air. As he did so, his head and shoulders were instantaneously forced against the top of his turret, causing him temporarily to lose consciousness.

Curly, meanwhile, instinctively reached for the throttles, pushing all four levers forward for full power, believing it would give them a greater chance of surviving the collision. Rusty, the skipper, momentarily lost control, the great machine which ordinarily required no little physical effort to fly suddenly and terrifyingly 'going limp in his hands' as it rode piggy back on the other Lancaster. Rudders, elevators and ailerons were suddenly rendered useless for what seemed an eternity as Rusty fought to maintain level flight.

Elsewhere in the aircraft, the rest of the crew were reporting in, shaken but otherwise in control, demanding to know what was happening. Ted, the Special Duties Operator, was one. Ted was used to being kept in the dark – quite literally – as the eighth man of the crew busy with his radio jamming equipment in a special compartment behind the Navigator's and Wireless Ops stations. With no windows, his was a solitary world and he seldom saw anything during a flight. Instead he would concentrate on his 'special' task, only leaving his post on the rare occasion, as a trained gunner, to relieve one of the other crew. It was his 24th Op. An old hand.

As well as the 'thud', Ted knew something was seriously wrong because of the unusual smell. Not the familiar and almost comforting smell of a Lancaster, or the more sinister smell of cordite from a shell exploding too close nearby, but something different altogether. The smell of burning rubber.

Ted switched on his intercom to ask Rusty what was happening, but by the time he had done so, one half of the tragedy at least was almost over. The two aircraft intertwined, seemingly in one final, grotesque embrace of death. Then the other Lancaster slowly fell away, skidding at a 45 degree angle out of control, disappearing into the cloud at 2,000ft. Harry, floating in and out of consciousness, was aware of the stricken bomber being pulled inexorably by the forces of gravity closer and closer to the ground. He was willing the crew to get out. But not a single parachute was seen.

Then, as so often happens after a moment of such intensity, everything seemed to happen in a rush.

Norman, the bomb aimer, quickly launched into a conversation with his pilot about the airworthiness of the aircraft, and in particular the state of the bombs and the bomb doors. They knew they were damaged, but just how badly? Norman reported all of his instruments u/s, and a rapid decision had to be made. Ted was aware of the Aldis light being shone in his general direction; it was Norman, working his way carefully back along the aluminium fuselage, examining the bomb bays and the 13,000lbs of Medium Capacity explosive which had miraculously survived the impact and continued to cling, albeit precariously, to the belly of the Lancaster.

That the bombs had not been hit had been their first piece of luck. Now they had their second. Although severely damaged, it was still possible to open the bomb bay doors. The hydraulics were operating sufficiently and to the best of his knowledge, Norman felt confident he could jettison the bombs over the target. Rusty accepted the word of his bomb aimer. Discipline amongst a bomber crew was everything. It was this discipline, and the trust which each crew member had for the others' expertise that had saved their lives on more than one occasion, and would be tested to the limit again. Rusty did not hesitate. Checking with the rest of the crew he announced his intention to carry on to the target. They had come this far. Better get it over with rather than return and risk the chance of it not counting as an 'op'.

Having been unburdened of their uninvited guest, Rusty had by now regained control of his aircraft. The aircraft was responding to the controls, although a little sluggishly. Later he might have problems, he knew, and landing was likely to be a bit dicey. The undercarriage was bound to be damaged, but for now he counted his blessings. They were alive, and A Wing and a Prayer (seldom had an aircraft been more appropriately named) was still flying. But for how much longer?

It was now only eight minutes after the collision – although it must have seemed like hours. Checking once again on the crew, and Norman in particular, he prepared as he had done many times before for the bombing run. The gunners swept the night sky, very much on the qui vive for nightfighters. This was the most critical moment.

Norman crawled through to his position, lying flat on his stomach, looking downwards through the Perspex blister. Approaching the target, the transmission from the Pathfinder's Master of Ceremonies could just be heard calling in the Main Force to 'bomb the flares'. Not all of the message was audible, however. Indeed only moments before, some of the aircraft had already been instructed by the MC to return with their bombs and in the event only 39 of a force of 126 Lancasters and six Mosquitoes would 'successfully' complete the operation, and overall the operation was deemed a failure. Fortunately, none of this could be known to A Wing and a Prayer and her crew.

Rusty held the aircraft steady as Norman called out the bombing instructions, albeit with some difficulty, and counted down to the target: " 30 seconds … 20 seconds … 10 seconds." The tension was palpable. Visibility over the target was not good. A thick haze was obscuring the engine sheds and marshalling yards, although Norman thought he could just make out some flares and railway lines in his Mark XIV bombsight. It was enough. The aircraft was holding up well. A glance at his compass told Rusty he was maintaining a course of 128 degrees magnetic and a quick check of his ASI read a constant speed of 180 mph. The thin white needle of his altimeter told him was also maintaining height.

Norman continued 'flying' the aircraft through his bombsight, calling out the last series of adjustments to his pilot, waiting until the wires crossed the aiming point until at last he shouted out the words they had all been waiting for: "Bombs Gone". They held their breaths. Would the bombs release? They were about to find out.

It was one minute past midnight. Only 10 minutes had elapsed since their collision. Each of the 11 one thousand pounders and four 500 pound bombs fell away from the underside of the Lancaster without incident, tumbling through the night sky in their trajectory of death onto the target 12,000ft below. Norman checked and re-checked there were no hang-ups.

Lightened of its load, the aircraft characteristically 'jumped' as Rusty turned away from the target, and opened the throttles, his flight engineer at his side. Alec, the navigator, calmly called out a new course for home as their bombs exploded through the haze on the target below.

The first leg of their journey was over. The easy part. Now they had to get home.

1. EARLY DAYS

Ted was still at school on 3rd September 1939 when the Prime Minister Neville Chamberlain mournfully announced to an expectant nation that the country was again at war with Germany.

Like many 15 year olds brought up with stories from the Great War, he greeted the news with a mixture of excitement and trepidation. This time around, however, people were less prepared to believe that the war would be over by Christmas. Ted might well have been in a hurry to 'do his bit', but for the time being at least, his age stood immovably and incontrovertibly in the way. The war would have to wait.

Born in Birmingham, Ted's early education was spent at his village school in Bourneville. An aptitude for learning, and specifically an interest in the sciences, gained Ted a coveted place at Kings Norton Grammar School, a prestigious establishment well-known in the local area for its thorough education.

Passing his School Certificate in 1939, he chose, not surprisingly, Physics, Maths and Chemistry to take as Highers and all three subjects were to serve him well in the period immediately after school as an apprentice mechanical engineer. But it was three years studying the German language that was to have such a dramatic impact on his life, and the conduit to a very 'special' tour with Bomber Command.

But such adventures were still some way off as Ted left Kings Norton in 1941 and started his apprenticeship with one of the major local employers, the Austin Motor Company.

Now after many re-incarnations long-since lost within the Rover Group, at the time the Austin Motor Company was one of the premier motor manufacturers not just in the UK, but also the world. An apprenticeship was much sought-after, and promised a steady career and certain future for the youngsters of the age. At least that had been true before the war. Now, nothing could be so assured.

Austin occupied the same massive site in Longbridge as its successor does now. The story goes that the company's founder, Herbert Austin, 'found' Longbridge after numerous exploratory cycle rides around Birmingham. Situated some seven miles from the City, he found a small derelict printing works that proved to be just what he wanted. Friends came forward with financial help, and the Austin Motor Company was born.

That was in 1905, and within a year the first production model was rolled out, the 1906 Austin 25/50 hp Endcliffe Phaeton. Herbert Austin tested the vehicle himself, and was extremely satisfied. So were his customers. Skilled workmen soon found their way to Longbridge and in the first full year, 270 of them turned out 120 cars in the original 212 acre factory. Expansion and extensions continued and other cars were added to the range. Austin coachwork came to be admired and as respected as much as the dependability of the chassis.

By 1908, nearly 1000 workers were employed and a night shift was found necessary. More additions were made to the factory, and an output of 1000 cars a year was planned. By the outbreak of the First World War, the business had expanded into manufacturing industrial and marine engines, and in

February 1914, the business changed from private to public ownership, with capital increased to more than £50,000. Within months of the First World War being declared, Austin shifted manufacturing from cars to munitions. Rapid expansion of the Longbridge site became inevitable, and by 1917 had trebled its size and even had its own airfield. Employee numbers – including now many women – reached more than 22,000 at its peak.

During the war, Austin produced more than eight million shells along with 650 guns, 2,000 aeroplanes, 2,500 aero engines and 2,000 trucks.

Between the wars, the success of the company continued, setting new standards for automotive manufacture and design around the world. Herbert – by then Sir Herbert – Austin continued to test many of the cars himself, including the first Austin Seven which although greeted initially with ridicule in some quarters, opened a new era in motoring. The Austin Seven became the most popular small car in the world, and was even raced by the great Malcolm Campbell, ultimately becoming the first 750cc car to reach a speed of 100 mph in England.

Immediately upon the outbreak of the Second World War, the company began producing a number of articles for the Nation's war effort. The variety and quantities of articles produced were staggering. More than one and a quarter million rounds of two, six and 17-pounder armour-piercing ammunition and twice the number of ammunition boxes were produced.

Jerrycans, steel helmets and bomb casings were made in their thousands, as well as suspension parts and driving gear units for tanks. And still the factories produced wheeled vehicles of various types, to a total of more than 36,000. The shadow factory at Crofton Hackett, which started production with Fairey Battle light bombers and Mercury and Pegasus aero engines, ended by turning out Lancaster heavy bombers.

When Ted arrived, therefore, in 1941, it was to a very different Austin Motor Company that had existed between the wars. But it was nonetheless demanding. His experiences there were many and varied. "They made sure we worked in every part of the plant. We were meant to spend four months in each department: the machine shops, the gearbox shops, engine shops and so on. We also spent time in the drawing office and service department, learning as much as we could about the business."

During this time Ted was also studying at the Birmingham Central Technical College from which he later graduated as a fully-fledged automotive engineer.

A less glamorous aspect of his job involved six months in the foundry, employing his new-found skills shovelling sand. Whereas to some, sand shovelling is a noble occupation, to Ted it was an incongruous departure from his learning up to that point. In the last few months he spent with the company he lost more than two and a half stone in weight. It was a bit warm in there.

By now, Ted had celebrated and passed his 18th birthday, but again his eagerness to get into the war was thwarted by his job which was still listed as a 'reserved occupation.' Even as a sand shoveller. There were, however, two 'escape' routes open to him: aircrew or certain categories of the navy.

It seems ironic reading the plethora of exciting (and occasionally excitable) autobiographies and biographies published during and since the Second World War that many have been driven specifically to the Royal Air Force by a desire to fly. To them, there was simply no other option. They had more than likely had their first taste of flying in an old first world war trainer as a glorified fairground ride, and been bitten by the bug, never to look back. Ted was different. Since he had never fancied sailing, the RAF was his only choice.

In the full knowledge that he would never be called up if he stayed where he was, Ted opted to leave his 'safe' occupation, and in October 1942, with Charlie Bliss, one of his best friends from work, journeyed down to the nearest recruiting office to volunteer for aircrew duties; his goal to be a pilot. He didn't know if he would be any good at it, but it had to be better than his present circumstances, and he would at last be 'doing his bit'.

By this stage of the war, the RAF had very much 'got its act together' in terms of the processing and training of new recruits. At the outbreak of war, the RAF possessed an operational strength of 2,600 aircraft and 173,958 officers and airmen. By May 1945, these totals had risen to 9,200 aircraft and 1,079,835 RAF, Dominion and Allied Officers and airmen, of whom no less that 193,313 were aircrew. Specifically in Bomber Command – the Command in which Ted would ultimately serve – the headcount rose from 14,280 through to more than a quarter of a million by 1944.

In October 1942, the time at which Ted volunteered, the air force was a very different beast than it had been at the outset: bigger, more organised, and more sophisticated both in its aircraft and its needs. This increased sophistication had led to the emergence of several new categories of aircrew (or 'trades'). Still the aircraft required pilots, of course, and observers, although the responsibilities given to this particular trade were subsequently divided between Navigator and Bomb Aimer (or to be accurate Air Bombers) to form the nucleus 'PNB' group around which each crew was built. (An official PNB scheme was introduced in the Summer of 1942). But other specialist trades began to emerge: Wireless Operators, Air Gunners (given a higher status and a higher rank).

And with the advent of the four engined bombers, the Flight Engineer came into his own. The options available to volunteer aircrew, therefore, were far from mundane (and so the WEA categories).

But if Ted thought the RAF couldn't wait to get their hands on young men of his calibre, or were desperate to have him in their ranks, he was to be sorely mistaken. Not surprisingly, given his recent exertions in the foundry, Ted had no problem with the medical examination at the local YMCA gymnasium. The Medical Officer examined him thoroughly with stethoscope and cold hands before signing the certificate that passed him as medically fit for active service in all categories, including pilot training. This was the first big hurdle out of the way. Many would-be aviators with a genuine passion for flying had been unable to do so because of colour blindness, asthma or flat feet. He knew, because he had already heard the stories, as had they all, and seen the disappointed faces.

His interview with the Aircrew Selection Board in Birmingham went similarly well. Why did he want to join aircrew? Where had he been to school? What was his civilian occupation? Whatever he said to the elderly members of the selection panel, and whatever he answered in the basic written tests he was given, it was clearly what they wanted to hear. The result was a recommendation that he be trained as a pilot. But then came the disappointment. Much to his chagrin, the RAF didn't seem to be in any hurry to train him. They had a backlog of volunteers, especially pilots, that meant it would be many months before he would be finally called-up. He was told to go home, and wait until he heard from them. A fine way to treat a would-be hero!

Ted took the news of his 'deferred service' stoically – as well as any 18 year old could. He would have to dig-in for the long run if he was to fulfil his new-found ambition to become a pilot.

For six months, until the Spring on 1943, Ted continued working at the Austin Motor Company, each day waiting for the envelope to arrive with the note that would tell him where and when to report, and that his services were at last required. Day dragged into interminable day, and week into long week until one morning Ted made up his mind. He wouldn't be a pilot after all, he'd do something else. He'd done more than his fair share of waiting, the war was now in its fourth year and if he didn't get into it soon it might all be over. (Indeed Charlie, his friend from Austin with whom he originally volunteered and who ultimately qualified as a Navigator never did see active service.)

Although pilots and navigators in particular were taking months – and in the event years – to train, other 'trades' could be taught more quickly and volunteers were in shorter supply. One such trade, was the Air Gunner.

Until that time again Ted had no predilection to Air Gunnery. Given his background and his education, he might have been better suited to another trade, such as flight engineer. Was he being impetuous? Was he being naive? The answer is yes to both of these questions, but it is invidious to attempt to judge Ted's position then compared to a war of today. Now with the advent of the modern media, live links and very graphic depictions of death and destruction, few would see war as an adventure in the same way that an 18-year old would have done so in 1943. Even given the horrors of the Great War, if you can't 'see' it, somehow it becomes that much less tangible.

The horrors of war were therefore a long way from Ted's mind as he wrote to the Air Ministry to volunteer as an Air

Gunner. The response was swift, and by return. But the official letter took a little time to find him.

The love of Ted's life at that time took the shape of a BSA 500 motorcycle and side-car combination. The bike itself was a dream, but the torpedo-shaped open side-car left a great deal to be desired, and every passenger was soaked to the skin or frozen to the bone depending on the time of year. It was, however, Ted's pride and joy, and every spare moment was taken up travelling around the countryside or visiting friends. It was while he was staying with one such friend, Geoff Brown, another apprentice at the Austin Motor Company, that the letter finally arrived. It had been sent to his parents in Kings Norton, and forwarded to Geoff's parents' home in Harrogate, where Ted was staying.

Lying on his bed on the Monday morning, Geoff's mother knocked on his door and entered brandishing the magical buff envelope containing the letter he had been waiting for.

The note told him to report to the Aircrew Reception Centre in London, where he would receive further orders. He was told to bring certain specific items with him – his National Registration identity card, civilian ration book etc – and of course his gas mask, and they had even kindly attached a railway warrant for his journey. At last the Air Force had seen sense. He was on his way.

Ted set off back to his parents to collect his belongings and headed for London. The train journey to the City passed in a blur. Everywhere around him men in uniform crammed into the carriages, some smoking, laughing, talking, others quiet with their own thoughts. The journey was slow but uninterrupted. The risk of attack by a marauding German aircraft was slim. It had been for some time now. Indeed it was the Royal Air Force who were attacking the German railway networks now as the tide was very slowly beginning to turn in favour of the Allies.

London was London, a Metropolis of unique sounds and smells; damage from countless Luftwaffe bombing raids still evident on scarred and missing buildings. From the station Ted took the bus to St John's Wood and the Aircrew Reception Centre which he was delighted to discover was based within Lords Cricket Ground. It was an incongruous sight to see hundreds of men in RAF blue queuing and milling around the prestigious home of cricket. The sound of leather upon willow was now replaced by career NCOs attempting to show their civilian 'rabble' their first taste of military discipline.

For a short time, Ted was billeted rather splendidly in a block of flats on the North-side of Regents Park, flats which had long since been requisitioned by the military 'for the duration'. The cookhouse was located in the zoo – a zoo now devoid of most of its animals who had been evacuated, like the City's children, to safer climes. Only the monkeys remained. It seemed somehow appropriate, and the irony was not lost on Ted or his fellow course members.

His life in the lap of luxury – or at least the best that war-torn England could muster – did not last long however. Having been issued with his kit, taught the rudiments of standing to attention, and suffered the usual dental checks and a blood-grouping session, the first part of his 'de-civilianisation' was completed. Ted now set off with his new-found comrades-in-arms to the station and via LNER on the 200 mile journey to the East coast of Yorkshire for the second part of his indoctrination. The Initial Training Wing (ITW).

Every member of the Royal Air Force – and indeed the military as a whole – had to have the obligatory period of 'bull' and 'square bashing'. They spent a minimum period learning how to march, stand to attention smartly and study classroom subjects, which often had to include the English language as well as hygiene and sanitation, air force law, aircraft recognition, principles of flight, engines, armaments, Morse, meteorology, navigation, and many other topics.

Ted's new home was the beautiful seaside resort of Bridlington. A big favourite with the Edwardians, the town had undergone a transformation at the start of the 20th century and now boasted the Spa Royal Hall, a new Town Hall and 400-yard promenade. Not long after war had been declared, the town had undergone a transformation once again, with many of its buildings requisitioned by the military and its civilian population of some 22,000 swollen by the ranks of newly-enlisted men.

Ted's billet was in one of the mighty Terraced-Houses on the sea-front at one end of the town; the lessons were held at the other, such is the logic of much service life both then and now. Every morning he and his classmates would assemble and be marched along the sea-front to be further indoctrinated into the ways of the modern air force. To only casual interest to local residents – who had seen it all before – Ted's Flight was made to exercise on the beach. They would march down to the shore, their PT kit hidden under their greatcoats, and their skinny little white legs and army boots contrasting ridiculously against the blue serge.

Marching back, depending on the time of day, they would invariably stop at Riley's Cookhouse to get some sustenance back into their bodies. Situated at the top of a flight of stairs, they would have to wait patiently at the bottom until those at the top had finished and come down before they could go up. It was somehow very typically militarily chaotic, but few complained.

Even in those early summer months of 1943, the weather in Bridlington could make it a bitter, inhospitable place with the cold winds blowing in from the North Sea across Flamborough Head. But if the outside temperature was anything to be concerned about, the temperature of the water itself was decidedly chilly.

The one part of their training greeted with almost universal dread was 'dinghy drill'. By this stage, the instructors had perfected the art of dinghy drill to Machiavellian proportions. The pier, which had once created so much pleasure in the happy days before the war, now became a nemesis. A volunteer was always called for to push the dinghy away from the pier. Ted soon discovered that the warmest place to be was actually in the sea. Cadets had to jump off the end of pier into the water and clamber into dinghy below. But in getting off the pier, they also had to avoid getting themselves tangled in the rather nasty birds' nest of barbed wire that had previously been erected as an anti-invasion precaution. Needless to say, not all of the cadets managed to make it in one piece. Torn flesh and damaged pride bore testament to those who didn't quite make it – but were made to do it again until they got it right.

Soon, but perhaps not soon enough, the initial training was completed, and what Ted considered the 'real' training would begin. From ITW, the various trades were scattered all over the country to receive their specific training, and Ted learned to his delight that his next posting was to the Elementary Gunnery School in the small town of Bridgnorth.

Bridgnorth, which Ted knew well from his various cycling expeditions as a youngster, is a small Shropshire town of 5,000 inhabitants, bounded on the east by the River Severn. From the 16th and 17th centuries, the town had established itself as a foremost manufacturer of woven carpets, but held its reputation for lace and stockings. Latterly, boatbuilding had flourished in connection with the barge traffic on the Severn. Now these genteel occupations had been exchanged for a new trade: training people to fight.

The 'Elementary' in Elementary Gunnery School was an appropriate word. There was seldom a gun in sight. For two weeks, Ted was shown photographs and silhouettes of every aeroplane then in service, and some that weren't. German aircraft, British aircraft, Italian aircraft, Russian aircraft, American aircraft, even Japanese aircraft. Ted was to learn everything about 'aircraft recognition' there was to know. There was no point teaching someone how to shoot down an aircraft if that aircraft ended up being friendly! Ted was bombarded with facts about wing spans and dihedral; about tail fins and engine housings; about maximum flying range and estimated fire-power.

Nothing was easy – the instructors saw to that. They had photographs of aircraft taken from almost impossible angles. Ted recalls only silhouettes, but in some cases, it was rumoured, they even had photographs of British planes with German markings, just to fool those who had previously relied on looking for an RAF roundel. Some made up their minds: if it didn't have four engines, they'd shoot at it no matter what! Ted struggled initially but got the hang of aircraft recognition over time. To start with, it was a complete mystery. And then one day, quite literally, it came to him, and from that moment on it became 'easy'.

One consolation at Bridgnorth was that much of the 'bull' that Ted had now grown accustomed to had disappeared. There wasn't so much shouting. The only RAF who still seemed bothered by 'bull' were the under-training (u/t) Wireless Operators who were also stationed there. Ted reckoned they had the shiniest brass of anyone he had ever encountered!

Another consolation was that it was only a very short course, and very soon Ted and his colleagues were again travelling across blacked-out Britain from Bridgnorth to Birkenhead, en-route to the next stage of their training and a more advanced gunnery school.

Arriving in Birkenhead, the Docks had been heavily bombed, and still showed much of the signs of damage that the Luftwaffe had inflicted two years earlier. The Docks around Birkenhead and particularly Liverpool had been a key focal point for many of the vital convoys coming in from the Atlantic, and the Town was a hive of activity. Ted and his colleagues were directed to the ferry terminal, an area that years before had been the scene of happy farewells and excited children. Here they boarded an Isle of Man Steam Packet Company vessel that would transport them to the island and Andreas, home of 11 Air Gunnery School.

The crossing was uneventful. The Irish Sea, which can pick up a squall to rival any of its more famous counterparts, was unusually but thankfully benign. Five hours on the ferry passed pleasantly before the tiny castle that denoted the sailors refuge came into sight and beyond it the port of the island's capital, Douglas.

The personnel were quickly and efficiently disembarked and stood, for the most part for the first time, on an island that would become their home for the next three months. The seafront in Douglas which tracks the natural course of the waterline is typical of many such large conurbations dotting the British coastline. Its splendid, imposing homes and hotels dominate the skyline, curving away, climbing gradually and disappearing into the distance. Douglas would become a focal point socially for Ted and his crewmates in the weeks ahead, but for now there was little or no time for sight-seeing. Almost immediately they were packed onto a five-tonner and driven North over Snaefell – the highest point on the island – to Andreas.

Andreas was a relatively new RAF station, and a satellite to the perhaps more well-known station at Jurby, which for a time became a second Cranwell famed for its officer training. Built towards the end of 1940, the first RAF personnel arrived in the Summer of 1941, and by October 1941 the first aircraft – Spitfires of 457 Squadron – began to operate patrolling the Irish Sea as part of No 9 Group Fighter Command. The influx of personnel was generally well received by the local populace, although relations were strained when the stately 120ft tower of the Andreas Parish Church had to be reduced in height by half to lessen the hazard to aircraft taking off from the main runway!

Despite this early setback, the village took the station to its heart, and did all it could in the way of hospitality to make everyone happy. Clegg's stores and Rainer's café established their reputations for providing the finest cups of tea and sticky buns; more substantial meals could be found in many a home where airmen were welcome and who, in return, provided cheap labour at harvest time.

During the Spring of 1943, a new role was found for the excellent facilities at Andreas, and preparations began to set up 11 Air Gunnery School of Training Command. The new Commanding Officer was Group Captain Mackay, an ex-Royal Flying Corps pilot who was universally respected and who would remain at Andreas for the duration of the war.

Ted arrived in the first few months of the Station's new role and was quickly thrust into its training regime under the watchful eye of the Chief Gunnery Instructor, George McKinley. George, a Warrant Officer who was subsequently commissioned, was a near miraculous character to the new intake, having survived 46 operational sorties in the earlier stages of the war when Bomber Command losses were reaching their peak. To have survived at all was considerable; to have survived as an air gunner especially was considered exceptional. George's 'boss' at the time was the Officer Commanding Training, Squadron Leader Toombs. He would be later succeeded by Squadron Leader J.C. Cunningham.

There was little similarity between the Elementary Gunnery School and the environment in which Ted now found himself. Certainly there was the same emphasis on aircraft recognition, but now Ted experienced a new level of training which every day brought the reality of war just that little bit closer.

The gunnery course consisted of 10 weeks intensive training for intakes of 30 arriving at fortnightly intervals. It comprised a series of lectures and practical sessions (ground training) before taking to the air. Now Ted added to his aircraft recognition skills with training on sighting, pyrotechnics, clay pigeon and 25-yard shoots, care and maintenance of weaponry, turret hydraulics, manipulation and operation, and the use of cine-camera guns. He learned how to strip a Browning machine gun – literally and metaphorically – blindfolded, and put it back together again.

The training huts were equipped with the various types of turrets then in use, including the Boulton & Paul Types A and F (as used on Halifaxes), and the Frazer Nash 121 turrets installed in Lancasters and Wellingtons. Most if not all of instructors were experienced aircrew, chosen to pass this experience on to the keen, fresh-faced hopefuls arriving every other week.

Greatest emphasis, not surprisingly, was placed on Air-to-Air firing. Clay pigeons and rifle ranges were all very well, and vital to teaching the basics of the mysteries of deflection shooting for example, but seemed far-removed from the 'real' thing. Air experience was gained, exclusively in Ted's case, on Anson gunnery trainers fitted with Bristol turrets as used in Blenheims. The pilots, Ted recalls, were invariably Polish, although communication was never an issue.

The ubiquitous 'Faithful Annie' – as the Anson was affectionately known – would be later replaced by Wellingtons, but for the time being they served their purpose with honour. Their only drawback, as far as Ted was concerned, was that they frequently seemed to require their undercarriage to be lowered and retracted by hand – and that task always fell to Ted. He also remember vividly on more than one occasion his pilot 'losing' the island in the mist that could quickly descend, and a 'hairy' trip or two back to base.

The would-be gunners in the Anson had to have something to aim at of course, and some way of measuring their success. The solution – albeit a primitive one in the context of today's high-tech generation – was to fire at a 'drogue', trailed in the sky by a 'tow' aircraft.

The drogue was a long, sausage-shaped object like an enormous wind-sock that was dragged through the air about 100 yards behind its 'host' aircraft. Target towing duties were undertaken by Martinets, a sturdy workhorse powered by a Bristol Mercury engine giving 850 hp and the only aircraft used by the RAF that had been specifically designed as a target tug. The distinct roar of the engine and the garish yellow paintwork adopted on the underside of each aircraft became a familiar sight as the aircraft and training crews went about their daily business, stooging across country to the designated firing ranges over the sea at both sides of the Point of Ayre (on the Northernmost tip of the island).

It would be fair to say that target towing duties to a highly-trained, highly-qualified RAF pilot was probably the nadir of his career. Indeed it was said that such a role was often meted out as a punishment. That's not to say they did not perform a vital role, or that they weren't in any risk. On more than one occasion, an over-excited air gunner kept his finger on the trigger a moment or so too long only to rake the target tug as well as the drogue with 'friendly fire'. Ted himself succeeded in shooting the tow-rope, rather than the drogue, much to the annoyance of all concerned as the drogue fell uselessly away and the aircraft turned for home after a 'wasted' trip. (Whether this was by luck or design is easy to gauge, but Ted maintains it was still a good shot!).

Once each exercise was complete (typically each flight lasted one hour), the Martinet would fly low over Braust and release the target. How they came to measure the accuracy of each gunner was remarkably simple. The ammunition they were given was dipped in printer's ink; it was then simply a task of counting the holes, and informing the gunner how many of his precious rounds had missed!

Contemporaries interestingly differ considerably in their opinions over this method of 'scoring'. There is the now famous tale of a well-known air gunner and later author who tells of a wager with his friend on one such air firing exercise. He detached a number of rounds from the ammunition belt and bundled them over the side to fall into the sea. His friend did fire at the drogue, but nowhere near the target, and with his guns depressed down at the water. When the results were promulgated, the former was credited with 60% hits on target, but his friend only rated 30%!

The one element that was perhaps the most exciting – and the most realistic – of all, were the Fighter Affiliation exercises, with Spitfires provided by the neighbouring fighter squadrons. Rather than aiming at an imaginary aircraft with real guns, Ted aimed at a real aircraft with an imaginary weapon, in the guise of a cine-camera gun.

The cine-camera gun was an ingenious camera-based device which took film footage as the gun trigger was depressed. Upon landing immediately after the exercise, this footage was then reviewed and analysed to see how accurate the gunner's aim had been. The camera never lied, and there were genuine gasps of astonishment amongst the gathered few in certain cases at just how wide of the target they had been. The friendly fighter would have been in less danger had they been firing real bullets!

The difficulties of air gunnery could not be underestimated. Hitting a 300mph fighter executing quarter cross-over attacks (passing at high speed from one side to the other), beam attacks, and attacks from behind was far from easy, yet had to be mastered. It took time; in Ted's case, a little short of 20 hours flying time before he was considered proficient.

But it was not all work and no play at Andreas. Station entertainment was laid on in the form of regular dances featuring Andreas' own musical ensemble, and visits were also made by Jack Hart's Jurby Band. To go further afield, Crennell's luxury coaches were available for a night out in Ramsey, where the Pool Ballroom was a popular venue and the Plaza and Corner cinemas provided the latest films. There was a definite demarcation between those pubs favoured by 11 Air Gunnery School, and those frequented by the fighter boys (no doubt with their top tunic button still undone) of neighbouring Jurby. There existed a healthy rivalry between the men of Andreas and the airmen at Jurby; unlike Jurby, however, Andreas could boast its own pub.

One particular feature of visiting Douglas was the return transport. The rail link from Douglas to Sulby featured steam trains more at home in a children's books by Reverend Awdry, and even if the train had left the station, it was reckoned that if you could still see it, you could probably still catch it!

Another memory of Andreas and the Isle of Man overall, was the food. The Isle of Man is internationally renowned for its Kippers; naturally being an island, fish were still in good supply and the smoking houses thrived. To airmen used to rations of a country that had been at war for more than four years, it was a welcome – even luxury – addition to their diet.

Soon, perhaps too soon, Ted's time at Andreas was coming to an end. Abruptly, like hundreds before him, and thousands after, his course had reached its conclusion. A final examination – with a distinction of 86.2% – and a hastily assembled passing-out parade saw Ted awarded the coveted single wing, with the letters 'AG' surrounded by a laurel wreath at its root. Also confirmed was his promotion to Sergeant, with the three chevrons indicating the minimum rank then given to aircrew, and always the cause of much disquiet amongst the 'regulars' who had often served for more than 20 years before achieving such exalted status.

Ted was now a qualified air gunner. Better than this, his assessment, signed by Squadron Leader Cunningham, earmarked him as an 'Above Average' air gunner, and 'a good worker'. Just how good, Ted had yet to really prove. But his time was rapidly approaching. By the 22nd October 1943, his training as an air gunner was complete. He now had to be trained to operate as part of a crew, and for this purpose, the RAF had devised a series of Operational Training Units (OTUs). And it was to 14 OTU in Market Harborough that Ted was posted.

For most of the war, OTUs were equipped with twin engined aircraft which until 1942 had been the mainstay of Bomber

Command. Typically they flew three marks (the Mk I, Mk III and the Mk X) of the famous Barnes Wallis-designed Wellington – the beloved Wimpy. It might also have an odd collection of battle weary Hurricanes (for Bomber Defence Training), Ansons and even Martinets for good measure (coded with the Squadron identification letter AM).

Moving to multi-engined aircraft was a big hurdle to surmount for the aircrew – and especially the pilot – usually because they were bigger and more powerful than anything encountered previously and partly because of the environment in which they would train. Prior to this point, many of the pilots had learned their trade in some far flung corner of the Empire – South Africa or the USA for example – with vast areas of desert or scrub without a single road or railway line. OTU training missions were over densely populated country with hundreds of roads, railways, villages and towns, unpredictably (although typically English) foul weather and the omnipresent fear of enemy aircraft.

For Ted, and his counterparts arriving at Market Harborough on that cold October morning in 1943, it was a strange experience. Until then, he had largely only mixed with his own kind, wearing the familiar single wing brevet of AG for Air Gunner. Now he encountered N for Navigator, B for Bomb Aimer as well as the double wings of a pilot. This motley collection would now be invited to crew up.

How these airmen came to 'crew up' varied enormously from OTU to OTU: some would be marched into a hangar and simply told to get on with it; sometimes the process was achieved in more convivial surroundings at the local hostelry. It was definitely unscientific, and would most certainly not be allowed today. How, for example, could a 19 year old assess the true worth of someone on whom his life may depend? Regardless of the rights or wrongs of the system, it worked, albeit with a few amusing exceptions and some which unfortunately had more fatal consequences.

Selection, in Ted's case, started with the pilot trying to team up with a navigator, then the bomb aimers, then the wireless operator and finally the gunner until he had a full crew. They would add to this crew with a further gunner and a specialist Flight Engineer once they graduated to the four-engined aircraft at a Heavy Conversion Unit. Ted found himself in the crew of a young sergeant pilot called Harper.

Forming part of 92 Group with its headquarters in Winslow, 14 OTU was designed specifically – as the initials suggest – to prepare aircrews for war. Operating from the airfield on the outskirts of the town, life consisted primarily of cross country flying, fighter, anti-aircraft and searchlight affiliation exercises (called 'Bullseyes'), and lectures, lectures, and when time permitted, more lectures. There was some time set aside for recreation, and generally the atmosphere was still more relaxed than they had been used to.

Sometimes, however, their 'training' was no less dangerous than those already in action. Indeed Arthur Harris, Commander-in-Chief Bomber Command had pressed several OTU crews from Flying Training Command into service early to make up his first 1000 bomber raid on Cologne on May 30th 1943.

Not unusually they were called upon to stooge about the night skies of Northern France, either as diversions to the main bombing effort to fool the German Radar plotters, or to drop propaganda leaflets on a receptive French audience (so-called 'Nickel' raids). It was similarly not unusual for these aircraft to return home having sustained damage from flak or fighters, or having suffered mechanical problems. Some aircraft – and their crews – simply disappeared.

The Unit's others tasks also included helping with Air Sea Rescue searches. Rarely were they ever successful. It was a vivid reminder to all on the station of the dangers that lay ahead, and no doubt contributed to a high turnout for Wet Dinghy Drill Training. During his time at OTU, Ted also successfully completed his Decompression Chamber test, whereby aircrew were 'taken up' to an equivalent height of 30,000ft and starved of oxygen. As the 'altitude' increased, Ted was give a series of simple written sums to complete, as well as signing his signature. Only when he safely 'landed' and saw the spidery scrawl that dominated the notepaper and the pathetic attempt at mathematics was the true lesson of oxygen starvation driven home.

Despite the increase in tempo of their training, Ted was still impossibly anxious to get into the war, lest it should be over before he had had a chance to 'do his bit'. Forever, on his own admission, looking for a short cut to the real thing, one morning he spotted a notice pinned to the information board that looked like it could be the answer. The notice was intriguing in its content, and vague in its detail. It was perfect. It asked simply for volunteers with a knowledge of the German language. It didn't say anything more than that. It gave no indication of what they might be volunteering for.

With all the hallmarks of a lamb heading for the proverbial slaughter, albeit with its eyes wide open and acknowledging it spelled trouble, Ted put his name down. It was, after all, only four years since he studied German, and only two years since he had left Kings Norton Grammar School, and his grasp of the grammar and the vocabulary would need only a day or so revision to be back up to speed.

For all his hopes, even Ted could not have imagined just how fast events were about to unfold. In less than a month he would be flying his first operational sortie. His 'first' crew, under Sergeant Harper, would be subsequently posted to No 9 Squadron at Bardney and shortly after lost on operations. Ted had been particularly friendly with another gunner, 'Lenny' Parker – an old-school pal. At the time he wasn't to know. And he didn't know the station or the Squadron to which he was posted. The station was Ludford Magna. The Squadron was 101. It was to be a very special posting, as he was about to find out.

2. SPECIAL DUTIES

Ted left Market Harborough on 26th November 1943, only six weeks after arriving from Andreas. He had never heard of Ludford Magna, and knew nothing of 101 Squadron. He was in for a shock on both counts.

After a short spell of leave, the day dawned for him to take transport to his new home. It was 1st December. Having ridden through the unfamiliar Lincolnshire countryside in an all-too-familiar five-tonner, his first impressions of his new home were the same as everyone else. Not for nothing was the station universally known as Mudford Stagna (or variations on a theme). The airfield, situated between Louth and Market Rasen, was not a permanent station, with all the luxuries that afforded. Ludford was temporary, with temporary accommodation, temporary facilities, and to a large extent temporary aircrew fighting what they hoped would be a temporary war.

The station had been built hurriedly (within 90 days) by the firm of George Wimpey at a total cost of £800,000 on farming lands previously owned by the Hilldred family. Despite being the highest point in Lincolnshire, Ludford became notorious for its muddy conditions, and was described by the station's first Commanding Officer – Group Captain Bobby Blucke – as: "a joke in very bad taste played by the Air Ministry at our expense." Blucke, who became somewhat of a living legend to all those who served with him, was not a man to mince his words. Few disagreed.

Ludford opened for business in June 1943 with the arrival of the first aircraft from 101 Squadron, previously based at Holme-on-Spalding Moor. Later it would add FIDO to its list of 'special' facilities, a means of dispersing fog by burning thousands of gallons of petrol through pipes laid the length of its runway.

The crews were not encouraged by what they saw. In their hurry, the contractors had omitted to install perimeter or runway lights, so some of the arriving aircraft had to taxi by shining an Aldis lamp from the bomb aimer's window. Conditions were so bad, that they found themselves living amongst shovels and cement mixers. Despite all these obstacles, however, the Squadron was soon operational. Its commanding officer, Wing Commander George Carey-Foster (a regular officer later to have an eventful post-war career in the Foreign Office at the height of the Burgess/Maclean scandal) was keen to press on, and 101 was back in business for an attack against Mulheim on 22nd June.

101 itself already had an established tradition as one of the RAF's first night bombing squadrons having been formed at Farnborough in July 1917 and glorying in the motto: *Mens agitat molem* (Mind over matter). Operating in France for the last year of the war, it took part in a number of night raids on enemy camps, communications and supply lines all over northern France and Belgium. Disbanded shortly after the war (a casualty of the 1920s equivalent of today's 'peace dividend'), the squadron was reformed in 1928, being amongst the first Squadrons to operate the Blenheim light bomber 10 years later. With the outbreak of the Second World War, 101 again found itself in the thick of the action, attacking barge concentrations in the Channel Ports. Converting to Wellingtons in 1941, it assumed its night bombing mantle, and took delivery of its first Lancasters in October 1942.

Ted was delighted to have been posted to a Lancaster Squadron, to have the opportunity of flying in the aircraft that was to become arguably the single most important Allied aircraft of the Second World War.

Long before the war had started, the Air Ministry had laid down plans to replace the twin engined aircraft with four engined 'heavies'. The first aircraft to enter service was the Short Stirling, which although at first doing outstanding work, and considered a pleasure to fly, was to prove a bitter disappointment in the longer term. A low operational ceiling, in part due to its short wing span (reputedly cut short because the wings on the original design would not fit inside a standard RAF hangar), meant the casualty rate soared, and – with some exceptions – it proved an unpopular aircraft with its crews.

The second 'heavy' to enter service was the Halifax, from the stable of the redoubtable Frederick Handley Page, an aircraft from a respected designer which was continually modified until it became in most respects a fine aircraft. (It is described by the author Max Hastings, somewhat unfairly, as 'a workhorse with no breeding'.) The first 50 were in service by January 1942.

The third to become operational, the Lancaster, had an inauspicious not to say disastrous start. Originally a twin engined aircraft and called the Manchester, although simple to build and maintain, its power-plant (the ill-fated Rolls Royce Vultures) proved dangerously unreliable, more aircraft being lost from engine trouble than enemy action. Modifying his design around four Rolls Royce Merlins, the designer Roy Chadwick created the legend that was the Avro Lancaster.

The Lancaster had a cruising speed of 216 mph, and could carry twice the bombload of an American B17 Flying Fortress. It could transport a crew of seven (eight in 101's case) 1,660 miles at a ceiling of 20,000ft. As well as the bombload, armament consisted of twin .303 machine guns in the nose and dorsal turret and four .303 machine guns in the tail turret. It was, in almost every respect, a thoroughbred amongst thoroughbreds. It was also extremely successful. As early as July 1943 it was noted that 132 tons of bombs were dropped for every Lancaster lost on operations. This compared with only 56 tons for each Halifax lost, and 41 tons for each Stirling. By March 1945, there were no fewer than 56 squadrons of Lancasters in first line service with Bomber Command. By the war's end, Bomber Command had 745 Lancasters ready for operations and 296 in the Operational Conversion Units.

Until this time, 101 with its Lancasters had been every inch a 'conventional' bomber squadron fighting a 'conventional' war, if war could ever be described thus. But behind its 'ordinariness', 101 was assigned to 'Special Duties'. It held a big secret. Just how big, Ted was soon to discover... and sooner than he anticipated.

Ted's suspicions were first aroused by the fact that they were not introduced to any other members of the squadron. They were kept separate, as though contagious with some highly infectious disease that required their isolation. Ted was to become used to such isolation, and throughout his tour did not billet with any of his crew. (His pilot later revealed it was in case he talked in his sleep and gave secrets away; at least that is what they had been told).

Looking around him in the obligatory Nissen hut in which they had all been assembled on arrival, the impact of what he had actually volunteered for began to sink in. Although the detail was initially scant, it was very clear to everyone gathered that they had arrived at an 'operational' rather than a training squadron. The lack of 'bull' was once again palpable, and even the aircraft appeared to have a more menacing, imposing air. They looked different, as indeed they should, as each aircraft also had three large, odd-looking aerials protruding from the fuselage, two on the top (one almost in line with the main spar and the second in front of the mid-upper turret) and the third underneath to the right of the bomb aimer's position. Each aerial was about five feet in length, streamlined in section, four to five inches wide at the base tapering to about two inches at the point where there was a short section about six inches long and approximately two inches wide. These curiosities were, as yet, unexplained.

Ted did not know at this stage that there was to be little or no honeymoon period, and that in less than a month he would be flying his first sortie over enemy territory. What was also clear was that he and his colleagues had three distinguishable things in common: they were all RAF, they were all volunteers, and they all spoke German. It wasn't true to say they were all of the same nationality. Most, certainly, were British, but there was also a fair smattering of aircrew from the Colonies including a French Canadian and an Australian. Neither was it true to say that they all spoke German with the same degree of confidence or fluency. But again, those with such 'obvious' German names as Fischl, Wilkeman, Krieg, Beutel, Woeflfe, Marks, Buringer and Schwartz were perhaps at a slight advantage.

Happily the wait to discover their fate was not a long one. The very next morning, the new arrivals were again herded onto a truck and taken to Louth to board a train that would take them to a secret establishment 'somewhere in England' (actually in Kingsdown, Kent). Here all would be revealed. But for the time being, it was still a mystery.

Arriving at the training facility under tight security only heightened the sense of expectation. The new recruits sat patiently, as though back at school, waiting for the master to tell them they could turn over their exam papers. And then it was explained. In simple terms, Ted and the others had volunteered to operate one of the first airborne electronic counter-measures ever to be used operationally. Fundamentally, it meant listening in to German nightfighter controllers and preventing their instructions getting through. But perhaps a fuller explanation is required to better understand the significance of Ted's new role…

Throughout 1942 and 1943, Bomber Command had played a deadly game of Cat and Mouse with its German nightfighter counterparts. Technological development was the order of the day. For every new measure one side introduced, it was only a matter of time before the other had developed a suitable countermeasure and was again on the offensive. How the Germans were structured, with their Tame Boar and Wild Boar tactics of controlled or freelancing fighters will be covered elsewhere; what the Germans relied on, however, was to receive timely and accurate information on the position of the bomber stream. Thwarting the controller became a key objective. Knock out the controller and the fighters were effectively 'blind'.

The first British initiative was to establish 15 ground stations that transmitted a wall of sound over the VHF frequencies the Germans used. This, for some bizarre reason, was called 'Ground Cigar', and although successful, had one major drawback; its range. The answer, clearly, was to devise a way in which this same concept could be taken into the air. As luck would have it (war forever seems to be as much about luck as design), the Telecommunications Research Establishment at Malvern had been working on a similar device, codenamed 'Jostle'.

Air Commodore Sidney Bufton, a distinguished 'Bomber Baron' and then Director of Bomber Operations, laid down the requirements for the 'Jostle' carrier on 23rd April 1943.

"The aircraft required must be capable of proceeding with the main force to the target in order to provide protection. As enemy aircraft may home in on to the jammer, the aircraft must have the performance to give a sufficient degree of immunity from interception. It has to be a heavy aircraft to accommodate the equipment."

The obvious choice was the Avro Lancaster.

The Lancaster was, by a large margin, the most suitable aircraft to attempt Bufton's experiment. Having chosen the aircraft, the next hurdle was to find a suitable squadron. How 101 came to be chosen seems so unlikely it almost has to be true. It was originally decided that the honour of carrying Jostle should go to 100 Squadron at Waltham. Then it transpired that 100 squadron had already been earmarked for the installation of another piece of 'secret' equipment – H2S. Since the aircraft's power supplies could not cope with Jostle and H2S together (indeed this was to become a problem later in the war), it was decided to fit Jostle into a different squadron. The next on the list was 101!

With the change in squadron came a change in name. 'Jostle' was replaced in favour of 'Airborne Cigar', which itself was universally acclaimed and acknowledged, even at the highest level, as 'ABC'. And so the ABC aircraft and the ABC squadron was born.

Meanwhile, Ted listened to the specialists describing their new equipment intently. Its application was officially described thus:

"ABC is designed for use on bombing raids over enemy territory to interrupt enemy communications by jamming particular frequencies on which radio messages are being sent to night fighters from ground control stations. It comprises three 50-watt transmitters, each capable of sending

out frequency-modulated jamming signals covering narrow frequency bands selected within the 38.3 to 42.5 Mhz range by means of manual tuning controls. A 'panoramic' receiver provides means of locating enemy transmissions in this range of frequencies, and setting jamming signals accurately upon them."

More detail was to follow:

"The total weight of the equipment is 604 3/4lbs. When the equipment is switched on, all three transmitters are suppressed simultaneously while the panoramic receiver sweeps over the 38.3 to 42.5 Mhz band 25 times each second. Any signals picked up are displayed on a three-inch diameter cathode ray tube. Here the frequencies are represented as a horizontal line, and any signals picked up are shown as vertical 'blips' which grow out of the base. When a 'blip' appears, the operator sets a bright strobe spot to mark it, and 'throws' a switch which stops the panoramic sweep of the receiver; he tunes it to the single frequency marked by the strobe and brings his earphones into the receiver circuit so that he can listen to the incoming signal. Having identified this as an enemy ground transmission, he may then switch on a transmitter and turn the tuning control until the jamming signal, as displayed on the cathode ray tube, covers the marker spot. The enemy signal is then completely obliterated in his earphones by the output of the jamming transmitter.

"Whenever desirable, the operator may suppress the transmitter in order to determine whether the enemy has changed to a new frequency, and if so, re-adjust the jamming signal. Three transmitters are provided so that three communications channels in the enemy Ground Control Intercept (GCI) band may be simultaneously jammed."

So all was clear. The mystery of the three aerials spoiling the otherwise beautiful lines of the Lancaster had been explained. The RAF needed people to operate this equipment, people who could recognise an R/T transmission as being definitely German. Ted began to appreciate just how important his school qualification had become.

In actuality, the real level of knowledge of the German language was not especially important. It was being able to distinguish between other languages – Czech, Polish Russian etc – that was key, as well as understanding a few specific words that the enemy night fighter controllers used, for example 'Kapelle' for target altitude and 'Karussel' for fly an orbit. Much has been made of these 'Special Operators' and their 'spoofing'; again in reality, neither Ted nor any of his colleagues were ever asked to transmit 'duff' information. This was not their role. There role was simply to drown out the fighter control frequencies with noise.

Whilst some struggled, Ted had no trouble getting to grips with the new technology. Indeed he found it easy. Like his gunnery training that must have seemed like years before but was in fact only weeks, the equipment soon worked to his deft touch. A little more practice back at Ludford then find himself a crew and he'd be on his way.

Whilst Ted was busy completing his Special Duties training, Flight Sergeant Russell 'Rusty' Waughman and his crew were busy integrating themselves into squadron life, flying a series of cross-country exercises to familiarise themselves with the local area.

The seven men with whom Ted would share his ultimate adventures had arrived on the squadron a few days before. They might have arrived sooner, had Rusty not had a few problems at the Heavy Conversion Unit (HCU) and Lancaster Conversion Unit (1662 at Blyton – another primitive airfield built for the duration and with little thought for the comfort of the men) keeping the aircraft straight on take-off. This had delayed their passage on to 101. Although Rusty would later describe the Lancaster as 'The Queen of the Sky', initially he had some difficulties. His legs were – and still are – on the short side, in fact a quarter of an inch too short for flying according to a post-war RAF medical. He therefore did not quite have the reach to get full control quickly, and struggled as a result. Also having a fist-full of four throttles took some getting used to.

Five of the seven – Rusty, Norman 'Babe' Westby (bomb aimer), Alec Cowan (navigator), Idris 'Taffy' Arndell (wireless operator), and Harry 'Tiger' Nunn (rear gunner) had been together since OTU at Wymeswold, flying Wellingtons. At HCU, they picked up another gunner, Tommy Dewsbury, and a flight engineer, Len Riches. Four engined 'heavies' were technically more complex, with more engines, more associated dials, controls and fuel, plus items such as retractable undercarriages and associated hydraulic systems. They also had additional armament in the guise of a mid-upper turret to protect the aircraft from beam attack, hence the need for additional crew.

The crew was a good mix of characters and temperaments, with diverse backgrounds and experiences. What they shared, primarily, was their youth, and an inner self-belief that they were the best. Rusty (20) was a pupil surveyor from a working class family in the North East. He was generally viewed as 'unflappable' by his crewmates – the kind of temperament you needed from a man in whom you entrusted your life; Alec (20) was an office clerk from London and, as would be expected from a navigator, was very precise; Norman (20) had been brought up in a gypsy-like environment and was a keen swimmer. All he had ever wanted to do was join the RAF. Despite – or maybe because of – his bohemian past, he was always immaculately turned out, and in direct contrast to Taffy (20), the whirlwind from the Valleys who perhaps cared little for his appearance or for what others thought of him.

Harry (20) was a Canadian volunteer whose father had an undertakers business in Vancouver. He was particularly fond of Jazz, and was never very far away from his beloved clarinet which he would practice with alarming obstinacy. Len (20) was a trainee engineer, a very private individual who had to date proved more than competent in training but whose performance on operations would shortly jeopardise the lives of the entire crew. The only married man amongst them was Tommy, who at 26 was very much the 'old man' of the crew, whose wife Alice was expecting and who suffered considerable good-natured leg-pulling as a result.

The crew had gelled together from the start, although there was initially some reluctance from the wireless operator, Taffy, to join up. On the day of 'crewing up', Taffy and a good pal of his Colin 'Ginger' Farrant (another wireless operator from Lancing) had a date to keep in Loughborough. They decided between them to hide out in the toilets until the selection process was over. Allowing plenty of time to go by and believing themselves to be in the clear, they emerged from their hiding place only to be confronted by two pilots.

"Are you two crewed up?" asked the older one of the two, a 23 year-old Sergeant pilot called Twitchett.

"Yes," replied the recalcitrant w/ops in unison, attempting to bluff their way out.

"We don't believe you," came the reply, "and we're both short of a wireless operator. We'll toss for it."

And so they did. The younger man, Rusty, lost the toss, giving the taller pilot first choice. He opted for Ginger, believing the fresh-faced youngster, on first appearances at least, to be the more intelligent and reliable of the two. He may have been right, but was never really given a chance to find out. They were posted shortly afterwards to 12 Squadron at Wickenby and went missing on their first operation on the night of 5/6th January on a long haul to Stettin. Colin Farrant, who was only 17, had clearly lied about his age to 'join up', and paid the ultimate price. Rusty, meanwhile, was stuck with the fiery Welshman, a decision he never regretted, but that would on occasions push his even temperament – and that of the rest of the crew – to the limit, sparked primarily by Taffy's fondness for beer.

Rusty had specifically requested a posting to 101 to join a pal who he had met whilst training, Paul Zanchi. Paul was a tall, angular young man from Southend-on-Sea who was well-known for his fiery personality. His Flight Commander informed him that 101 was a 'special' squadron and only the best were sent there. The fact that 101 was so special gave them priority on crew availability; it also meant their loss rate was tragically high.

Rusty arrived on the squadron to discover that Paul's crew had become another statistic in Bomber Command's casualty figures. On the night of 26th November, Paul had been sent out to bomb Berlin on one of his first operations. He never came back. Miraculously, Paul's regular flight engineer – John 'Curly' Ormerod and wireless operator John 'Gats' Wetten – had not flown that night and so survived. 'Gats' was ill, and Curly had been sent home on special leave. More miraculously still, one of the crew who had been on the operation – the navigator John Jossa – survived, although badly injured, having fallen with the aircraft from 20,000ft. He and Paul had been arguing at the time, breaking one of the fundamental rules of survival – total discipline whilst in the air.

That night the Squadron lost three crews, the other two being Flight Sergeant Bennett and Pilot Officer Walker. Bennett's Lancaster came down at Heuchelheim, killing all-but two. Walker was shot down by Hauptmann Eckart-Wilhelm von Bonin of II/NJG I – a 39 victory ace and holder of Germany's highest award for gallantry, the Ritterkreuz – and crashed at Aywaille, 18 km south west of Verviers in Belgium. Walker and his navigator Jack Blandford survived, Walker to become a Prisoner of War and Blandford to be spirited away by local Resistance, eventually making it to Switzerland in April 1944. Arthur Walker and his crew held a fistful of medals between them for an earlier operation to Hannover in September. On the run-up to the target they had been attacked by flak and nightfighters and the port inner engine set on fire. A fire also took hold aft of the mid-upper's position. Walker dived to blow the fire out, whilst the Flight Engineer, Sergeant Stan Mayer feathered the engine and the gunners succeeded in keeping the nightfighters at bay. Mayer then went back to put out what was left of the blaze, but was overcome by fumes and had to be pulled clear by the mid-upper. Now on three engines, Walker assessed the damage. The intercom had been knocked out, the DR compass was smashed and the trimming cables burned through. His rear gunner was u/s, and he had had to jettison his bombs in the earlier dive so there was no point in going on to the target. The aircraft turned for home, arriving back in England on four engines thanks to Mayer who had managed to get the damaged engine re-started. The night's activities brought a unique award – Conspicuous Gallantry Medals (CGMs) to two members of the same crew – Walker and Mayer. The gunners, Hicklin and Scott – were both awarded the Distinguished Flying Medal (DFM), and there was a Distinguished Flying Cross for the bomb aimer, Flying Officer Gadd. It was a heavy loss to the Squadron.

On arrival at Ludford, and having dumped their kit in the obligatory Nissen hut that was to become their home for the duration, Rusty's crew reported to 'C' Flight led by a quietly-spoken 22 year-old Scot, Squadron Leader Ian Robertson. Although young, Robertson was already a veteran of many operations, sporting the diagonal purple and white ribbon of the DFC on his tunic – the result of a particularly outstanding action the previous August.

Robertson, at the time acting Flight Lieutenant on his 13th operation, had been returning from Nuremberg when both his starboard motors suddenly caught fire. He began losing height rapidly and almost immediately afterwards the port inner engine also failed. Down to only one engine, he gave the order to prepare to abandon the aircraft. Somehow he managed to regain control, only to discover that four of the crew had already bailed out. Only the navigator – Flying Officer Sid Kennedy – and flight engineer Sergeant Tom Calvert – remained. They didn't need anyone else. Calvert managed to get the starboard outer re-started and they headed for home at 6,000ft over enemy territory on two engines and with no flying instruments. God, luck or both were on their side that night for they made it back without further damage. Robertson and Kennedy were awarded immediate DFCs and Calvert the DFM.

'C' Flight was quite some distance from their hut, and being the depths of winter, the walk squelching across muddy fields and lanes (with such bizarre names as Fanny Hands Lane – so ludicrous it could not have been invented) was not particularly enjoyable. To call the 'C' Flight Office an 'office' would perhaps be overstating the case. It was again a hut, which was entered from one end to reveal the Flight Commander's desk on the right, and opposite that on the wall, the crew list board showing the availability of the crews for operations. From this the crews for the dreaded Battle Order were selected (i.e. those scheduled for operations that evening). Apart from the odd battered chair, there was little else in the way of furniture to give the office any sense of character or comfort.

After the training units, the squadron atmosphere and seeming lack of 'Bull' was again very noticeable. There were other differences, not least in the aircraft. As Ted had done, Rusty had also remarked on the aerials on the Lancasters, the two on top looking for all the world like a pair of clothes-line posts without the clothes line! He had noticed too, that standing on the ground it was possible to reach up and hold the aerial, but that if you did, you got a hand-full of grey-brown anti-freeze grease that took some time to remove. Needless to say, he only did it the once.

On 29th November, whilst Ted was busy training, Rusty got his first opportunity to fly one of the strange-looking Lancasters. That evening, having donned flying kit and drawn parachutes from the parachute section, they made their way to one of the furthest dispersal points (nicknamed 'frying pans' because of their shape) on one of the remotest parts of the 'drome for a six and a half hour cross country flight that had to be abandoned early as the weather closed in. Rusty was disappointed in returning early but delighted with the aircraft, a Lancaster III ME 565 coded 'W'. It was a significant meeting in many ways. The fortitude of 'W' – later christened A Wing and a Prayer – would later save their lives. It also introduced them to unforgettable characters within the second 'half' of the Bomber Command team: the ground crews.

The ground crew responsible for 'W' was led by Corporal 'Jock' Steadman. Jock had looked after the aircraft lettered 'W' for all of his time at 101, from early Holme-on-Spalding Moor days to its closure at the end of hostilities. He was certainly a lucky talisman for in all that time he only lost two aircraft.

It has been an unfortunate malaise that the ground crews, without whom the aircraft would never have flown and Bomber Command's strength might have been critically depleted, have never received the proper recognition they deserve. Other authors have tried; most post-war autobiographies pour worthy praise on their squadron colleagues and equals. And yet the harsh reality is that the role of a fitter, rigger, armourer etc, although fully acknowledged by the cognoscenti, still fail to capture the public imagination in contrast to pilot, bomb aimer or gunner. This is not to say, however, that their role was not without its risks, or its fatalities. Accidents whilst 'bombing-up', for example, were not so infrequent as to be considered uncommon. It is to their eternal credit that they took their status as 'extras' against their 'leading men' primarily without fuss, or complaint, and with tremendous character. For tremendous characters they most undoubtedly were, and few better to exemplify this view than Jock.

Rusty learned quickly Jock's occasionally unorthodox means. The aircraft was invariably parked facing away from the fence, so that when Jock and his lads – Nobby Burkes, Jack Fernley and Jock Scott – wanted their oily uniforms cleaned, they would dunk them in petrol, then hang them on the boundary fence behind the aircraft so that when the engines were run up on test, their overalls were dried by the slipstream. Jock also achieved notoriety for his unorthodox collection of unauthorised stores which were secreted in a dispersal hut he built beside the aircraft. This enabled him to effect repairs and patch up damage to the aircraft, so keeping the Lancaster serviceable and ready for action without delays or being grounded, thus keeping maximum availability for the war effort. Jock and his boys worked tirelessly, often all through the day and night to keep 'their' aircraft serviceable, only catching up on their sleep when the squadron was on a mission. The groundcrews were as much responsible for ultimate victory as their airborne colleagues.

But victory was still a long way off in that freezing winter of 1943 as Rusty, Ted and the others prepared themselves for the ordeal ahead, with the obvious concoction of apprehension, excitement and fear.

Three further flights for Rusty and the crew, as yet short of a Special Duties Operator, were undertaken on the 9th, 10th and 11th December – a cross-country flight with two fighter affiliation exercises either side. Such an intense period of training and an obligation in essence to fly at every opportunity was typical of the time. Soon, very soon, they would be declared operational and nothing could or would be left to chance. They had to be 100% up to the task, both in the eyes of the flight commander, and the squadron commander himself.

To this end, Rusty should have seen action in advance of the rest of the crew. At that time, it was customary for new pilots to fly a sortie as a second pilot – a so called 'Second Dickey' – with a more experienced pilot and crew. The idea was to provide the pilot with invaluable experience by watching and learning from others on an actual raid, and to iron out any potential difficulties before being let into to air with his own crew. Unfortunately, the pressure the squadron was under at the time did not always allow for such niceties, and Rusty's first taste of action was to be shared with his colleagues. (Rusty was later to become the Master rather than the pupil as his experience mounted and he became the 'old hand' of the Squadron, albeit that he proved a far from lucky tutor. All three of his 'Second Dickey' pilots subsequently failed to return, making Rusty somewhat of a jinx).

Following one further Bullseye flight – a substantial trip of more than six hours stooging around the enemy coast generally making a nuisance of themselves, Rusty and the crew were at last ready for their first operation. The date was 23rd December 1943. Rusty wandered over to the 'C' Flight Office, and then to the main Crew Room. This was in a larger complex of connected huts. On the right of the entrance, in the corridor on the right hand wall, was a notice board. Rusty glanced at the Battle Order for that night's operations. Listed across the top were the aircraft captain and crews – 17 crews in all, 136 men. Towards the bottom, to fly in aircraft DV 307 coded 'Z' Zebra, was the name of Waughman. Underneath, as well as a listing for any training exercises to be carried out that night, was a stern warning: "All crews not on Battle Order are to remain in camp until after take off." A time of origin was printed, and the Order signed by the Commanding Officer. Briefing would be at 15.00 hours. On the column on the far right under the title 'Special Duties' was the name of a man they had yet to meet, and who had yet to meet them. Sgt Manners. Ted.

Knowing that they were required for that night's operations (the squadron's most recent operation had been a six-hour trip to Frankfurt), the next few hours were spent in frantic activity. The crew assembled at their aircraft and went through a number of pre-flight checks followed by a short, 20 minute air test to ensure that everything was in good working order. Nothing was left to chance. While the aircrew went about their business the groundcrews and a host of other unsung specialists set about their thankless tasks.

Preparing a Lancaster for an operation took time and not a little sweat. The load for that night was to be based around a single 4,000lb high explosive cookie, 48 x 30lb bombs and 930 x 4lb incendiaries. All were taken from the bomb dump by the armourers and loaded onto their individual aircraft. As well as the bombs, they also had to check, re-check and re-load each of the Browning .303 machine guns – eight in all. This could involve feeding tens of thousands of cartridges into the ammunition belts and needed tremendous care. A single cartridge jammed in the breech at a critical moment could have fatal consequences for the gunner and his aircraft.

All over Ludford Magna, the groundcrew swarmed like a proverbial army of ants over their charges. Men were filling great 2,500 gallon capacity petrol bowsers and oil bowsers, each of which held 450 gallons. One Lancaster could take almost the entire contents of a single petrol bowser if required. Every point on the bomber was checked: engines, plugs, instruments, turrets, undercarriages, tyre pressures, bomb door mechanisms, and a host of other things, including the secret equipment. Nothing was – nor could be – overlooked or left to chance. Perfection as always was the watchword.

And it was not just the groundcrews who were stretched to the limit. The intelligence officers were working at double time, ensuring their target maps and photographs were up to date, and collecting the very latest information from Group. So too the meteorological officers revising up-to-the minute weather information from their own central channels.

Few at this stage new the target destination. Group had telephoned through early that morning with its request for a relatively modest raid on 'Whitebait'. Every German City had a codename, chosen by Harris' Senior Air Staff Officer Robert Saundby, based, it was said, on his love of fishing. For example Trout was Cologne, Catfish was Munich, Grayling

Nuremberg etc. Whitebait was 'The Big City', Berlin. The bomb load and H-Hour, as well as the target route followed in due course. First to be notified were the Squadron and Station Commanders, followed by the Flight Commanders and the various 'leaders': Armament Officer, Navigation Officer, Signals Officer, Bombing Leader, Engineering Officer etc. Each then concentrated on their own speciality. The crews – with the exception of the navigators who would be briefed two hours in advance – would not know the target until the main briefing, but already the old hands were guessing. A heavy fuel load meant a long trip, deep into enemy territory; a heavy bomb load and less fuel, a shorter trip, but no less hazardous. The type of bombs – cookies and incendiaries – also betrayed certain targets.

Having nervously eaten their 'flying meal' of bacon and eggs, the time for main briefing arrived and Rusty gathered his crew, making their way to the main briefing room. The room was large enough to hold all of the crews who were on operations that night, plus the odd skipper flying a 'Second Dickey.' It was a room typical of the period, furnished with trestle tables and chairs, with a raised dais at one end and as its main feature an enormous OS map of Western Europe. Being the newest crew, Rusty and the others lingered and worried about inadvertently taking the place of a crew of 'old sweats' and incurring their disapproval. Nervous chatter ceased and chairs scraped on the floor as the crews stood to attention with the entry of Group Captain King, the extremely popular Station Commander, and the Squadron Commander, with their Flight Commanders and entourage following dutifully behind.

Carey-Foster mounted the platform and called for silence:

"Be seated Gentlemen. Captains, answer your names. We'll start with 'A' Flight. Flight Lieutenant Rowland? Pilot Officer Nightingale? Flight Sergeant Langford? ..."

Each name read out was responded to in the affirmative. Some fidgeted in their seats, or dragged nervously on a cigarette while the formality was completed. Then the Wing Commander began talking about general matters, petrol, bomb load, take-off etc before calling for the Intelligence briefing. The senior Intelligence Officer (IO), Squadron Leader Thompson, took the lead, his billiard-cue-style pointer firmly in hand.

"Well Gentlemen, your target for tonight is the Big City, Berlin..."

The news was met with the customary diversity of responses, from sharp intakes of breath and whistles to looks of apparent indifference. It was not a surprise.

"Berlin as you know is the Capital of the Third Reich and claims to be the third largest City in the World with a population of about four and a half million and a population density about the same as London, i.e. about 12,500 per square mile..."

The minds of some who had already heard the briefing and raided Berlin before began to wander, their attention wavering until the information specific to tonight's operation was imparted.

"...The West and South-West areas are mainly compact residential quarters, while the North-West is occupied by scientific and military institutions, machinery works in the North and woollen factories in the North-East. To the South-East are the furniture and metal plants and in the South are the railway repair shops..."

The IO continued, Rusty and the others listening intently, mindful lest they missed something vital.

"...Berlin was last attacked in force on the night of 16/17th December by more than 480 Lancasters, and despite thick cloud it appears the raid was a success... Flak was moderate, with heavy flak experienced from 18,000 up to 20,000, and the searchlights fairly ineffectual, mainly because of the 10/10ths cloud over the target ... The fighters were waiting for us, with interceptions from the Dutch Coast and in the target area. Keep a sharp look-out, especially on the homeward leg... Make sure of your turning point after the target, or you could run into the Magedeburg defences..."

Many didn't need reminding about the flak or fighters. 101 Squadron had lost three crews on the last Berlin raid and six others since the assault on Berlin (The so-called Battle of Berlin) had begun a month before. Most of the 54 Lancasters lost on the night of 16th/17th November had been victims of crashes, with the majority of losses within No1 Group. Unusual weather conditions precipitating very low clouds meant many bombers were unable to find their way home. Not for nothing was that evening known as 'Black Thursday' in the annals of Bomber Command history.

"...you will be part of a force of 379 Lancasters, Mosquitoes and Halifaxes... Pathfinder Force technique is on the board here..."

At this point the IO pointed to a blackboard covered with cryptic information and codewords that to the uninitiated meant little, but to the more experienced foretold more of the difficulties they were about to face.

"...bundles of flares Red with Green stars will be dropped to mark the release point throughout. Main force should aim at the centre of all green TIs visible..."

With a last comment about decoys and Window (the strips of aluminium foil to disrupt German radar), the Intelligence Officer completed his lengthy diatribe.

"Any Questions?" he asked finally.

Somebody at the back enquired about convoys and intruders. Convoys had an annoying habit at firing first and then identifying whether the aircraft was friend or foe later. Similarly intruders, although doing a vital job protecting the bomber stream, were often shot at by their own side. A Ju88 and a Beaufighter in particular could be easily mistaken in daylight; at night, 100% recognition was virtually impossible.

The IO was followed by the Met Officer, who had the unenviable task of trying to guesstimate the weather forecast for the trip. "Tonight there will be cloud over the target area…" As he talked, he pointed to his own series of charts and graphs specially prepared for the occasion, and spoke a seemingly unique language peppered with the occasional word that the foregathered understood from geography lessons a thousand years ago. "… Synoptic situations … cumulus and strato cumulus … cold front closing in from the West …" For all the jargon, it meant trouble over the target.

Met completed his task and sat down once again, his place taken by the other specialists including the Flying Controller giving instruction on take-off, landing, and diversionary fields, and the Navigation Officer running through the set-course and turning point times for each wave. As each leader spoke, the corresponding specialist within each crew listened intently, scribbling occasional notes with information that could save their lives. Being new, Rusty and his crew took down virtually everything; later, with experience, they would learn to be more discerning. The Bombing Leader too had his own language, known only to others within his secret society. The Gunnery Leader was more direct, warning the gunners to swing their turrets and keep their eyes peeled at all times. He specifically warned them about attacks from below the tail which had been occurring with alarming frequency, and the procedures for evasive action.

With the briefing completed, crews were reminded to empty their pockets and synchronise watches. Emptying their pockets was vital so as not to give the enemy any means of information should they be shot down. A forgotten bus ticket or cinema receipt could betray a Squadron's whereabouts, or confirm a recent movement. Then with a final summary and word of encouragement, it was over, and individual crew members began to make their way to the navigational centre, bombing, gunnery and signals sections for their final preparations. As Rusty and the crew gathered in the crew-room, a tall, youthful young man approached and introduced himself:

"I'm your Special Duties Operator, Ted Manners. I believe I'm going to be flying with you tonight."

Rusty made Ted welcome and introduced him to the other members of the crew. The only member missing was Taffy, whose place had been taken by a Sergeant Bromley. Rusty was immediately impressed with Ted, and would later remark so in his diary, but the real test would come once they were in the air. The rest of the crew had already gelled nicely and had been together for some time, so it would be interesting to see how an eighth crew member would now fit in.

Each crew member then collected his own survival pack, comprising a First Aid kit (containing the inevitable morphine syringe) and flying rations wrapped in newspaper. There was the odd sandwich, Horlicks tablets, chewing gum and a large flask of tea which was filled from a large tea urn. They also received their Benzedrine tablets – the colloquially-named 'Wakey Wakey' pills which taken at the appropriate time would keep them awake and alert. (Some swore that the tablets had little or no effect on operations, but kept them pacing the corridors long after they'd landed when they should have been asleep).

Opposite the complex with the large Crew Room was the parachute section, one of only three brick buildings at Ludford, where the crews would collect parachutes and Mae Wests (life preservers), and the crews' locker room on the left. In the locker room was a series of tall metal lockers where each crew member kept his flying kit. The men began to dress: silk socks, fur-lined boots, thick pullovers and, for those lucky enough to have them, the treasured sheep-skin jacket. It was cold at 20,000ft, particularly for Harry in the farthest extremes of the aircraft, despite his heated flying suit. Only Taffy ever complained that he was hot, since the warmest place in the Lancaster was the wireless op station from where the heating would circulate. Having changed into flying gear, they each checked their head-sets and microphones in a test unit by the door, and then waited for the crew bus to take them to their dispersal. It was approximately 11-15pm; one hour before take-off.

For that night's operation, the crew would be flying in a Lancaster 1, DV307 coded 'Z' Zebra. Arriving at their aircraft, the eight men jumped out, and after Rusty had completed his external checks of the aircraft and exchanged a few words with the groundcrew they climbed on board, entering the Lancaster up a metal-runged ladder at the rear of the fuselage with Rusty at the lead.

When the Lancaster first entered service there was sufficient room for the crew to move about. But now with the aircraft packed with the latest technology from 'the secret war', space was of a premium. Each crew member made his way forward, clambering awkwardly over the aircraft's main spar in the process. This was a difficult enough exercise on the ground, but in the air, with an aircraft hit by flak, spinning, and with glycol spilling about the fuselage, it was a virtual impossibility.

In the cockpit, Rusty and Len, the flight engineer, began to run through the long series of pre-flight checks. In the front, Norman checked the escape hatch and the bomb aiming equipment as well as the front guns to ensure nothing had been disturbed since their inspection earlier in the day. He opened the small hatch leading to the bomb compartment and shone the Aldis lamp at the stores for one last check, then secured the packages of 'Window' ready for quick despatch over enemy territory.

Alec stowed his and Norman's parachutes under his chart table and then proceeded to lay out his pencil, rubber, ruler, protractor and other paraphernalia as if preparing for a School Maths exam. Immediately behind, the Wireless Op brought out his flimsies detailing the radio frequencies and colours of the day (a primitive identification method of firing coloured flares in a particular sequence to denote 'friendly') whilst behind him, Ted settled into his Special Duties position and began some preliminary checks of his 'secret' equipment. He, like the others, checked that the intercom was working properly and that the oxygen supply was flowing OK.

Further down the aircraft, Tommy and Harry looked over the guns and worked the turrets to ensure they were operating freely. Harry also stowed two empty beer bottles, ready to fling out over the target at the appropriate moment in his own personal gesture of defiance. It was a superstition that was always upheld.

Checks over, the eight men dismounted for a last minute pee. It was a bizarre superstition but many crews would urinate on the Lancaster's tail wheel before the off. Then, with the ritual duly completed, they would clamber back on board to await take-off.

It was very dark and very cold as all across Ludford Magna, 16 other crews performed the same essential tasks. Start-up time arrived. Trolley Accumulators ('Accs') were wheeled into position (Jock had managed to 'acquire' two just in case) to help start the mighty Merlins, starboard inner first (since this 'powered' the electrical systems within the aircraft) and then the others in turn until the four engines were singing their song of power in unison. A wave to the groundcrews, the chocks which had been restraining the aircraft pulled away, and Rusty inched the Lancaster forward onto the narrow perimeter track that would take them in single file on a winding path to the take-off position at the end of the runway. Rusty and his Flight Engineer continued their checks. Great care had to be taken when taxiing a Lancaster; it was not unheard of for a novice crew to run into the aircraft in front, or for the wheels to go onto the grass and get bogged down. Norman, who had already taken up residence in the nose, helped by shining the Aldis through the perspex, defining the edge of the tarmac.

Reaching the end of the track, Rusty turned 'Z' Zebra to line her up on the main runway. Here they waited anxiously for the 'green' from the Aldis lamp which would be their signal that it was their turn to go. As the aircraft in front slowly disappeared into the gloom, Rusty prepared, Len at his side, ready to throw the throttles forward for maximum power.

"Flaps Twenty."

Len checked: "Flaps Twenty."

"Radiators OK."

"Radiators OK."

"Throttles locked."

"Throttles locked," Len repeated.

"Rear Gunner, all clear behind?"

"All clear skip," Harry said.

Then it came. A soft blinking in the night. Their turn had come.

"Brakes off. Full power engineer!"

Rusty released the brakes and the aircraft trundled along the runway slowly at first and then gradually picking up speed. 30 tons of aircraft, men and ordnance travelling at 110mph and then defying the laws of gravity and taking to the air.

"Undercarriage up."

"Undercarriage up and locked."

"Flaps up."

"Flaps up," Len chanted.

Quickly the heavily-laden bomber was enveloped into the night, the only visible sign their small navigation light which was subsequently extinguished. Then blackness. It was just after midnight.

Within an hour, their first operation had descended into farce. Despite the best efforts of pilot and flight engineer, the Lancaster would not climb above 16,000ft. Gee, their principal navigational aid, went u/s, and similarly their Distant Reading (DR) compass. Despite the usual rugged dependability of both pieces of equipment, their failure, and the mechanical problems with the aircraft left Rusty no option. After only an hour in the air, and in the position 5250N, 0140E, the mission was abandoned. The bomb load, including the mighty cookie, were jettisoned safe in one of the pre-designated areas over water, and the aircraft headed for home.

They weren't the only ones experiencing difficulties that night. Pilot Officer Nightingale of 'A' Flight similarly had to abandon his operation when both the port outer and starboard inner engines failed. Otherwise the night had gone well for the squadron, and for the Group and Bomber Command as a whole. The poor weather conditions hampered the German nightfighter effort, and the fighter controllers were taken in by a diversionary raid by Mosquitoes over Leipzig. This meant that the bulk of the defending force did not arrive within the bomber stream until late in the raid, although they still accounted for 16 aircraft before the night was out. In return, the bomber force destroyed large parts of the south-eastern suburbs of the City, notably Kopenick and Treptow, with at least one crew – that of Pilot Officer Kelly – reporting "PFF (Pathfinder Force) first class. Attack well concentrated." The balance sheet was perhaps even.

It was a dreadful start for Ted, and indeed the whole crew. He had gone through, as they all had, all the emotions and anxieties of a first operation, and been thwarted by faulty equipment. There was nothing they could have done about it of course, but there was always the overhanging smell of suspicion for any crew returning early, especially those on their first operation. For the time being they would have to wait until they could prove to themselves – and perhaps to the others – that they had what it takes. Returning disconsolately to his quarters, Rusty took out his diary in which he had determined to keep a record of life on the squadron. For his entry for Thursday, 23rd December he wrote:

'Ops Berlin. Abortive. Gee and instruments unserviceable over channel. Not bad for first trip.'

After the last sentence he added three exclamation marks to denote the heavy irony of the statement. But one thing had gone right. The newest addition to the crew, his Special Duties Operator Sgt Manners, had made a positive impression and a promising start. Writing again in his diary, his entry for the following day, Christmas Eve, said simply:

'Special w/op Ted Manners. Hope to keep him!'

Christmas 1943 was nonetheless a happy affair for Ted and his new-found crew. Whether they would be his 'permanent' crew or not, he did not know, but he liked the characters, even the wild Welshman, and the calm authority that Rusty brought to his flying. There was already a good team spirit developing. Matters were helped further when on Christmas Day itself, all operations were scrubbed (indeed with the exception of 35 Halifaxes despatched on minelaying duties to the Frisians, the whole of Bomber Command was stood down). It was with tremendous relief that the all-NCO crew repaired to the Sergeants' Mess. Alec and a few of the others nipped off beforehand to the Airmen's Mess to help serve the traditional Christmas turkey with all the trimmings. Now they could escape the war for a few hours and share in the festive spirit, in the form of copious bottles of beer and the sight of the Signals Officer marching in and out of the tables playing his bagpipes! There was also the rare treat of fresh fruit, apples and oranges, as well as real coffee – a veritable feast.

As they sat, Rusty passed his menu around the table for the others to sign. Most took the chance to add a specific comment relating directly to their 'trade'. Tommy, the mid-upper, led with the advice: "Keep to the beam and you can't go wrong." Alec, the navigator, enquired, "What's your ETA?", whereas Harry, the rear gunner, reminded him "it's cold back here". Len, the Flight Engineer, signed his best wishes "with boost", but the last word went to 'Babe', the bomb aimer. He wrote laconically Rusty's epitaph: "Rusty Waughman – may he RIP."

Celebrations coincided with a change in the command structure at Ludford. 101 Squadron was part of No 1 Group, then commanded by the exceptionally gifted Air Vice Marshall E.A.B. Rice CB, CBE, MC. Edward Rice was a former solider who had transferred to the Royal Flying Corps and served with distinction in the RAF after the First World War. Although not as famous – nor as well-connected perhaps – as his near neighbour in No 5 Group The Hon Sir Ralph Cochrane, his achievements were nonetheless impressive. He always got the most out of his squadrons and was instrumental in trialling new payloads for each of his aircraft. The results spoke for themselves: Lancaster for Lancaster, No 1 Group aircraft carried a higher tonnage of bombs than any other group. It resulted, however, in higher than average losses, and none more so than in 101 Squadron. The proliferation of the Group, in line with the expansion of Bomber Command's strength, had extended the lines of communication to such an extent that it was fast becoming unworkable from a command perspective. The result was the introduction of the 'Base' Organisational structure.

As part of this Base structure, No 1 Group sub-divided its airfields into geographical cells (Bases), each of which was commanded by an Air Commodore. On 20th November 1943, approval was sought to create No 14 Base at Ludford with Group Captain Blucke as Base Commander. The proposal was formally approved on Christmas Eve 1943. Blucke now found himself in charge not only of the HQ and 101 Squadron at Ludford, but also 12 and 626 Squadrons at Wickenby, and No 1667 HCU at Faldingworth. He was a popular man, and it gave the Squadron something else to celebrate that Festive season.

War of course doesn't stop for Christmas and Bank Holidays, and 101 was shortly to find itself once again in the thick of the action. This time Ted and his crewmates would have better luck and an exciting trip – but the sort of excitement they could well do without!

On the morning of Wednesday 29th December, the call came through from headquarters and the codeword was once again 'Whitebait'. Berlin. A Main Force raid comprising some 712 aircraft, mixed Lancasters, Halifaxes and Mosquitoes. That the target was Berlin was rapidly becoming no surprise to the crews of Bomber Command. What they didn't know at the time, and was only later categorised as such, was that they were only a few short weeks into what was to become known subsequently as 'The Battle of Berlin' – a sustained effort by Arthur Harris to destroy the German Capital and so win the war. Harris maintained that the quickest route to victory was to destroy the morale – and the property – of the German people, as well as their factories and munitions of course. It was, in his mind, 'total war'. He wrote:

"We can wreck Berlin from end to end if the USAAF will come into it. It will cost between 400 and 500 aircraft. It will cost Germany the war."

He was to be proved wrong on both counts. In his letters and deputations to Churchill and the Chief of Air Staff Portal, he achieved only one half of his aims. Neither would press for the Americans to join Bomber Command's assault on Berlin, although Harris would later allege that he would never have embarked on the Battle had he known that the Americans would not be taking part. The Americans were committed to their own programme, 'Pointblank', which had as its target specifically German aircraft production. It was a plan to which all of the Western Allies had apparently agreed. Harris knew, but, history suggests, largely chose to ignore it and work to his own agenda.

How Harris got away with his own personal crusade to bring Germany – and specifically the Berliners – to their knees has never been satisfactorily answered, although a good many have tried. Certainly it appears he was never ordered directly *not* to carry out his plan, and it is largely accepted that he must have had the support – albeit surreptitiously – from his superiors, and most particularly Churchill. What is perhaps most surprising is that anyone really believed that Germany could be bombed into surrendering. And this has nothing to do with the benefit of hindsight; there is good evidence to indicate that many thought so at the time too. Goering believed that one of the keys to the defeat of Britain was the destruction of London. Destroy the spirit of the British people by destroying their capital. He failed. If anything, it made the population still more resilient. Why then should it work in reverse? Whatever the arguments, whatever the political machinations of the time, Ted and the rest of crew had little or no knowledge of what was going on. They simply did as they were told, and if ordered to go to Berlin, then to Berlin they would go.

The squadron offered 17 crews for the night's operation: six from 'A' Flight (led by Squadron Leader Marshall), six from 'B' and the balance from 'C' Flight. Take-off time was set for 17.00 hours. Taffy was still sick, so his place on the crew was taken by a spare 'bod', Sgt Melbourne. The briefing earlier in the day included details of the route, which would be a long approach from the South, passing south of the Ruhr and then within 20 miles of Leipzig. Mosquitoes would be flying diversionary raids at Dusseldorf, Leipzig and Magdeburg. The confusion resulting would cause the German ground controller inordinate difficulties in vectoring his fighters onto the bomber stream and most of the bombers would get through unscathed. However good the diversions, the fighters still found Lancaster DV 292 'Y' Yorker with Ted and his crewmates on board.

Ted had only just intercepted the first ground control transmission when the first attack came as they crossed the

Dutch Coast. And they were lucky. Harry in the rear turret just caught a glimpse of what he took to be a Junkers Ju-88 twin-engined aircraft attacking from astern and called for evasive action, opening fire at the same time, his four brownings chattering in reply. The Junkers made a sweeping pass, machine guns and canons blazing, but was successfully beaten off by the gunners and skilful flying from Rusty. But they were not out of it yet by any means. Approaching the target, Rusty held the aircraft steady as heavy flak burst around them, shell fragments clattering against the side of the aircraft. Norman, the bomb aimer, had been in the nose since take-off. Now this was his favourite part. They were five miles from the target, with a thick layer of 10/10ths cloud several thousand feet below. The cloud was illuminated by the ground searchlights, so that the cloud layer looked like a white sheet beneath them. Then Norman spotted something – a small black object silhouetted against the white cloud. He kept watching, fascinated, and just long enough to realise it was a fighter aircraft climbing towards them on an almost vertical flight path. It was a typical nightfighter tactic to climb vertically and rake the soft, un-defended underbelly of an aircraft, closing to 300 yards and firing the length of the bomber's fuselage.

Norman shouted: "Bandits, Bandits, single fighter attacking directly beneath. Range approximately 4000 yards and closing rapidly. Prepare to corkscrew port. Range 3000 yards ... 2000 yards ... 1000 yards ... Corkscrew port. Go!"

Rusty threw the aircraft into the classical evasive manoeuvre of the time, diving the aircraft to port as the fighter passed upwards to starboard, and then climbing sharply in the opposite direction. Corkscrewing placed tremendous strain on the aircraft's airframe and called for a super-human effort from the pilot, but it was nearly always successful in throwing a nightfighter off the scent. Corkscrewing over the target area, however, was even more hazardous, and seldom to be recommended. With upwards of 800 aircraft passing over a target areas in the space of 10 – 15 minutes, the risk of collision was very great indeed.

The FW 190 – a single-seat day fighter almost certainly on a *wilde sau* (free-range 'wild boar') operation – came in for a second pass but Rusty managed to lose him. The gunners fired again, the staccato 'rat-a-tat' just audible above the roar of the engines and the faint smell of cordite drifted to the front of the aircraft. The excitement had momentarily passed. Norman got on with the job of bombing the target, aiming at pyrotechnics red with green stars which had been previously laid by Pathfinder aircraft and continually refreshed with new flares.

"Bomb doors open, master switches on, bombs fused and selected."

"Hold her steady," Norman called to his pilot. "Isn't it lovely?" he added, engrossed in his job.

Norman had taken to giving Rusty a running-commentary on the colourful display around them. Rusty said nothing, perhaps slightly disturbed that Norman could ever see anything marvellous or beautiful in the pyrotechnic mayhem thousands of feet below. But each to their own.

Rusty had gained height to 19,800ft, and came in at a shallow dive, careful not to lose too much height, on a heading of 035M and at a speed a little over 150. Norman 'steered' the aircraft by instructing Rusty with a series of 'Left Lefts' and 'Rights' until he was satisfied with his aiming point. He pressed the bomb release in his hand:

"Bombs Gone."

The Lancaster noticeably 'leapt' as she became unburdened of the 4,000lb cookie and mixed incendiaries in the bomb bay. Rusty held the aircraft steady, waiting for the photo-flash to expend that would hopefully give them a successful photograph of the accuracy of their aiming point. The wait was interminable. It was only 30 seconds, but it was the longest 30 seconds of their lives. The Wireless Op confirmed the photoflash had gone. Then with the bomb bay doors safely closed, Rusty opened the throttles and banked steeply to port as Alec calmly called out from behind his curtain the course for home. It was 20.24.

The return flight passed without incident, although Rusty's instruments were by now u/s. Landing safely back at Ludford at a quarter past midnight, they were one of the last few aircraft to land. Many of the others had been home an hour since, had already completed their post-op interrogation and bacon and eggs, and had retired to their huts for a well-earned sleep. For the Waughman crew, that ordeal was yet to come, but they felt good that their first operation was now under their belt. The Intelligence Officer was quick, but thorough: "Did you see any fighters? Where were you attacked? Was the target obscured by cloud? When did the instruments fail...?" A long list of questions, all crucial to forming an accurate impression of the raid that could then be passed to Group and onto Bomber Command headquarters. A picture of a highly successful raid was fast emerging, with many of the other crews also reporting a successful attack and concentrated fires. Flight lieutenant Rowland, for example, who had landed an hour earlier had told the IO that he could see the glow from the fires 100 miles away, as did Flying Officer Todd and Pilot Officer Slater. Only one aircraft was missing – that of Flight Sergeant Shearer. News would later reach the Squadron that Shearer and six of his crew had survived as Prisoners of War (POWs), having crash-landed at Schillerslage, 4km from Burgdorf.

Whilst seven of the crew spoke with the IO and the various specialists present, Ted was separated from the pack for his own debriefing. Here they wanted to know specific details – frequencies scanned, number of broadcast intercepts, at what stage the first signals were detected and where, any technical problems encountered etc. Finally with the interrogation completed, the eight repaired to the mess – now virtually empty – for their bacon and eggs and then to bed. It had been an eventful day. They had proven themselves in combat for the first time, and despite a rough trip had made it through in one piece. Their traumas, however, were only just beginning.

Cowardice is not a pleasant term. In the Second World War the RAF had their own parlance – Lack of Moral Fibre (LMF) or 'Forfeiture of Commanding Officer's Confidence', both euphemisms for the same thing that brought shame on an individual, and potentially his crew and the squadron. It was dealt with swiftly and harshly, with none of the under-standing and tolerance given in today's world of Post Traumatic Stress Disorder and the counselling that goes with it. Those reported with LMF (or reporting themselves) were reduced in the ranks and removed from the squadron, some-times within hours. They were also stripped of their coveted aircrew badge. Whatever happened to these men subse-quently was rarely, if ever, truly known. What was important at the time, is that their 'cowardice', their inability to go on was not allowed to affect other members of the squadron.

LMF manifested itself in many different ways. 'Early Re-turns' were considered to be one of the most obvious and visible signs of a pilot or crew losing its nerve. Aircraft return-ing consistently with heavy damage was believed to be another indication, the inference being not so much that the pilot was afraid, but rather was losing his judgement with potentially fatal consequences. Some aircrew, otherwise excellent in training, simply couldn't cope with operations and 'froze' at their station, useless to man or beast. They wanted to go on, but they simply couldn't cope. These were perhaps the most dangerous, because their actions threatened not only their own safety, but that of the entire crew.

Len Riches, the Flight Engineer, was one such individual.

Hope that they would be stood down to celebrate New Year was soon dashed with orders once again that they were to bomb Berlin with a complement of 16 aircraft. It was to be a relative 'light' raid in comparison to previous attacks, with 'only' 421 Lancasters taking part along with a handful of Mosquitoes on diversionary raids.

To pass time before take-off, a crowd gathered in the Sergeants' Mess and a card school quickly developed. Soon, the American, Technical Sergeant E. Jones USAAF known to everyone as 'Tex' and who was flying on secondment to the RAF, was winning every hand. As his crewmates' wallets were depleted, so his became stuffed with notes until he had more than £100 in winnings. With the time of departure fast approaching, the card school finally broke up. Jones gave all of his money away.

"I won't be needing it," he said, with the air of a man who knew he would not be coming back that night.

It was to be a busy night for the squadron, and a bad one; it was to be particularly disastrous for Ted and the others. Over the target area, Berlin was once again obscured by thick cloud. 'A' Flight Commander Squadron Leader Marshall was once again having a successful trip, bombing the flares from a height of 20,800ft; Pilot Officer Fawcett was having similar success, seeing a fresh load of well concentrated TI's over the target from the Pathfinders and witnessing a large explosion in the target area. Ted and the crew, flying in Lancaster DV 264 'L', were having no such luck.

It began to go wrong two hours into the flight as they approached the Dutch Coast. Rusty could see on the dials that the oil temperature and pressure on one of the engines was increasing, and he was losing revs. The pilot was on intercom:

"Take a look at the starboard outer will you Len, it's running a little warm – probably an oil leak or something," Rusty called.

Len didn't respond.

"Len, the temperature on the starboard outer. What's happening?"

Still the Flight Engineer did not respond. Then Rusty's worst fears came true. A red glow started emanating from the starboard outer followed by the tell-tale lick of flame as the engine caught fire. Not a big fire at this point but the engine was losing power and the aircraft was starting to pull to one side.

"Len. Hit the extinguisher. Put the bloody fire out."

But Len did nothing. He crouched, rooted to the spot, deaf to what was going on around him in a catatonic state, cowering, unable to react or respond.

Now they were in trouble. If the fire was left for a moment longer, it threatened to engulf the whole engine cowling and the wing. Rusty had no choice. Compared to modern machines, the layout of the Lancaster was rather crude, although efficient – except for the fire extinguisher buttons and to some extent the propeller feathering buttons. The fire extinguisher push buttons were aligned on the far right hand side of the instrument panel, below the feathering buttons and realistically beyond the practical reach of the pilot (especially the starboard outer which was the button positioned farthest right). With his Flight Engineer useless, and the rest of the crew otherwise engaged, Rusty was going to have to feather the engine and put out the fire himself. Having switched off the power and the fuel to the Starboard Outer and throttled back, Rusty released his restraining harness, half lifted his small frame out of the seat, got his fingers under the spring-loaded covers and depressed the buttons that would hopefully free them from the serious situation they were facing. Rusty clambered back into his seat.

"Pilot to crew. We've got an engine fire. I'm going to dive, see if we can blow it out…"

Rusty eased the control column forward and the Lancaster's nose went down. Normally the Flight Engineer would call out the speed and loss in altitude so that the pilot could decide when it was time to pull up, but Rusty was on his own. He judged it to perfection, and after a few moments, the combination of the built-in fire extinguishers and the effects of the dive had dealt with the flames. The immediate danger had passed.

Now the decision again – whether to go on with one engine and one flight engineer u/s, or return to base. It was a difficult decision. This would be the second time in three operations that they would have to abort, and the wrath of the Squadron Commander would be keenly felt, but the risk of carrying on with Len was too great.

"Pilot to crew. It's useless to go on. Navigator, give me a course to steer for home as soon as you can. Bomb aimer, we'll jettison the cookie over the sea."

Norman responded in the affirmative; Alec replied a few moments later with a new bearing to steer for Ludford Magna as the crew turned forlornly for home.

Wing Commander Carey-Foster was indeed furious, and demanded to see Rusty on his return. Rusty expected a carpeting and he got it, but he could only explain to the CO the truth. Len wanted to go on – he wasn't a coward in that sense – but Rusty knew that the moment they crossed the enemy coast, Len would become a liability. He had no alternative but to request a new flight engineer. Carey-Foster was a reasonable man, but his mood was not improved by news that two aircraft were missing, that of Pilot Officer Bell, and the popular 'C' Flight Commander, Ian Robertson. Nothing had been heard from either crew since take-off, although Bell and two of his crew would later be reported as POWs and the navigator, Sergeant Bailey, would make it home. Robertson was not so lucky.

Robertson, from Renfrewshire, had only recently been promoted Squadron Leader. He had an experienced crew with four DFCs and two DFMs between them, including the faithful navigator and flight engineer who had shared his earlier adventures. All would be killed. Also to perish that night in the Robertson crew was the American rear gunner, T/Sgt 'Tex' Jones. He had been right; he had not needed the £100.

Their loss, and Rusty's failure, were in stark contrast, and the Waughman crew retired to their quarters disconsolate with the night's events. It was not a happy way to start the New Year for them personally, or for the Squadron.

That night, Rusty wrote in his diary:

'Ops Berlin. Abortive. Engineer deaf. Starboard outer on fire over Holland. Pretty useless to go on with Len. Best thing to do is get myself a new engineer.'

Things just had to get better. And fortune was about to smile favourably on them at last.

Len's departure was unsettling for everyone, but fate was kind in his replacement. Curly Ormerod, the flight engineer in Paul Zanchi's crew that had gone missing in November, had no regular pilot and had been flying as a spare bod (by the end of his tour he had flown to Berlin on eight occasions with no fewer than six different skippers – surely some kind of record). He already knew Rusty and the others because they had shared a Nissen Hut and socialised together from the earliest days at HCU before joining the squadron. The opportunity to team up again with a regular skipper was too good to miss, and with the CO's approval, Curly became the eighth member of the crew. As Rusty was to note in his diary entry for 4th January: "Managed to get Curly Ormerod as engineer. Ex Zanchi's crew. A good lad and I'm glad we've got him."

These words were to prove prophetic indeed. The 5th January dawned with a new target and a new name to many save the oldest hands in Bomber Command. Stettin.

Stettin was another long-haul at the absolute limit of a Lancaster's endurance. It signalled a minimum round trip of 1,260 miles. Because of the increase in nightfighter activity – and an increase in their success – routes to target were becoming ever more complicated and long, and for Stettin, Bomber Command crews could look forward to a flight of nine hours or more.

At briefing, the Intelligence Officer informed them that this was the first raid on Stettin since September 1941. Just short of 350 aircraft would be involved, primarily Lancasters with a few Halifaxes thrown in for good measure, as well as the customary diversions by Mossies to Berlin to keep the fighters away from the Main Force. Much of the vital war traffic with Sweden had to pass through Stettin. As the biggest port on the Baltic – and the port for Berlin itself – it was a target of the utmost importance. It would be blitzed.

It was a beautiful moonlit night, although the moon was both friend and foe to the bomber crews. Take-off went without a hitch as the Lancaster DV 389 coded 'P' with its heavy load of fuel and bombs climbed steadily into the night, and made for its assembly point over the North Sea. The aircraft was performing well, with Curly keeping a close watch on the dials and making small adjustments to ensure the engines were running smoothly, with minimum vibration and maximum fuel efficiency. It was a long trip, and he wanted to make sure he still had something left for emergencies. He was also mindful of the wager they had amongst flight engineers to see who could get the most out of their aircraft!

Rusty climbed comfortably at an Indicated Airspeed a little above 170 mph but began to experience difficulties with the control surfaces slow to respond and sluggish in his hands. Curly hauled himself up into the astrodome to see what the problem was and reported ice forming at an alarming rate on the wings. Icing provided a quandary. Because it affected the flow of air over the wing, the performance of the aircraft, especially in relation to lift, could be seriously impaired. In severe icing conditions, there was a very real danger the aircraft would stall, with potentially disastrous consequences. The other danger was that chunks of ice could break off and damage other sections of the aircraft. Curly kept a close eye on proceedings as Rusty continued the climb, making 23,000ft. The critical moment had passed. They had got away with it – at least for the time being.

Before crossing the Danish coast, Taffy passed Ted more flimsies with frequencies to scan. It was a quiet night for fighter activity. Indeed the 12 Lancasters from 101, interspersed throughout the bomber stream, were all having a relatively quiet night, with only a few transmissions being found and intercepted. The diversionary raids were working, with most of the German activity focused on the spoof attack on Berlin by a handful of cookie-carrying Mosquitoes.

The first Pathfinder flares began to go down, the familiar red and green stars. Marking was accurate, and the bombs that followed began to cascade down into the central districts of the City, with several large colourful explosions being noted. Curly was impressed.

"Come and have a look," he said to Alec.

Alec appeared from behind his curtain and was momentarily terrified by what he saw which was surely the work of Lucifer.

"Bloody hell!" he said, and disappeared back to the relative safety of his navigator's position. He was happier not to know what was going on outside.

As Norman's turn to bomb came 'round (he was delighted with the scene of the target, snow-covered on the western bank of the River Oder), Rusty was again experiencing difficulties with the aircraft, this time another engine failure.

Curly had noticed the revs dropping. The needle on the port outer rev counter was flickering and the oil temperature on the rise. Then the port outer packed up, just as they approached the target area. Flying on three engines was not a major concern. Height could still be largely maintained, and the aircraft could be trimmed to fly without foot load. The Lancaster could fly on two and even one for very short periods of time if required. It meant that they had to be careful with fuel consumption, however, and Curly set to work in redistributing the fuel to maintain maximum economy and minimum wastage. This was not as easy as it sounds. Climbing with a full load, a Lancaster would consume some 360 gallons per hour. Curly reckoned on getting one air mile per gallon at peak performance. Naturally at height the aircraft became more economic, but with one engine dead and the earlier problem with icing affecting the aircraft's performance

– not to mention other factors such as headwinds etc – he would have to be spot-on with his calculations.

With their bombs successfully despatched, Rusty turned for the long journey home, a flight that would be slightly more anxious now with a slight reduction in performance that would see them amongst the last to land. Rusty was now no stranger to landing on three engines. As he approached Ludford, he made a right hand circuit over the base, lowering the undercarriage and flaps to 20 degrees as normal. On final approach, with Curly's assistance Rusty was careful with the power, maintaining a steady 120 mph IAS, only winding off the rudder trim as he committed to land. With the three good engines performing well, Rusty brought the heavy aircraft down with a slight bump and squealing of rubber. They had made it. Curly's calculations had been bang on; there were only a few gallons left in the tanks, but they were safe and home. It was 09.00hrs, and the bacon and eggs had been well-deserved.

Between the 6th January and the 14th January, for several glorious days, the weather closed in and the Squadron was stood down. Whilst a handful of air tests, cross countries and practice bombing flights were flown, the squadron was ostensibly free, giving it time to play.

Like any young men, most of their free time was devoted to one thing: drink. The objective was to quaff as vast a quantity of ale in as short a time as possible. Any and every opportunity to get off-base was taken. There was a serious side to their otherwise debauched lifestyle in that it enabled them to bond as a team 'out of work' as well as on operations. To truly understand a man, his hopes, fears, ambitions, emotions, strength and weaknesses could one day save another man's life. Today this may seem a little melodramatic, but when a split-second decision in a bomber over Germany meant the difference between life and death, there was no margin for error. Trust had to be absolute.

For the next few days, Ted and the others shared a good few drinks, often as far away from the base as possible. Whilst the Black Horse and White Hart in Ludford held various attractions and were particular favourites, Ted liked to venture further afield to Louth, Market Rasen and Lincoln. Grimsby was also a popular destination, and in one pub, just off the main square, Ted and Rusty had the good fortune of getting to know some of the local fisherman. This translated into a regular supply of fresh fish, whenever time and availability allowed, which proved a great treat to supplement their otherwise dreary wartime rations.

Transport was always laid on in the form of a crew bus that would collect the aircrew – in various states of inebriation – and return them to base. First they would invariably visit the local Chippy, although the consequences of greasy fish and chips on a beer-laden stomach were inevitable. Also inevitable were the assignations – often far from discreet – that would take place on the back seats with the station WAAFs. It was always ever-so in wartime.

On one of the evenings out, one of their squadron colleagues missed the crew bus back to the station. Faced with getting a taxi or a very long walk home, the intrepid explorer opted for a third option that wasn't really available to him. He 'borrowed' an official station car. Congratulating himself, no doubt, on his initiative, when he arrived back at Ludford, the full horror of what he had done suddenly became apparent. In a fit of panic, he rolled the car into a ditch, and set it alight. Despite the demands of war he was caught, court-martialled and deservedly had the book thrown at him.

It is true to say that Ted and the crew shared everything together, and by everything, this included Norman's first 'operational sortie' with a woman. It was Taffy, of course, who took it upon himself to introduce Norman to the delights of the flesh. Taffy, ever the mischief-maker, had a friend in the Navy, based in Grimsby. One evening, with 'Gats' (Paul Zanchi's wireless operator who was not flying the night Paul was lost) in tow, the intrepid trio of Taffy, Norman and Gats set out to find 'Luscious Lil', a full-bosomed girl whom Taffy had taken a particular shine to for her tendency to wear a revealing outfit which buttoned up the front. The trio became a quartet, and the four crawled around the pubs in Grimsby and then back to Lil's for 'afters'. By this point, Norman was rubbing his hands with excitement, the sight of her black stockings with the thin black lines at the back making it almost impossible to bear. Needless to say, the evening concluded satisfactorily as far as most parties were concerned, and Taffy took great pride in his 'achievement' of turning a boy into a man.

Their period of respite was soon ended. An improvement in weather meant a return to operations – a new target and a new aircraft. It was to prove a happy union.

Friday 14th January dawned brightly. Not only had the crews of Bomber Command been rested, but so too the citizens of the towns and cities in Germany had enjoyed a period of relative safety to start their new year. The whirlwind, however, was only just beginning to gather pace.

For once there was some surprise at briefing when the curtain was drawn back to reveal the target – Brunswick. Their surprise was in itself hardly surprising given that Brunswick had never been subjected to a Main Force attack, and was not high on the list of potential targets when compared to such attractions as Berlin, Hamburg, Essen and Cologne.

Brunswick (Braunschweig) was an unusual choice in many ways. Situated 50 miles north-west of Magdeberg on the main railway line from Berlin, the region was primarily agricultural, with fine pastures and forests in the nearby Harz mountains which yielded fine foods and provided steady employment. The capital of the German duchy (Land) of the same name, Brunswick's population numbered just over 200,000 (1939 figure – 201,306 compared to a population in Berlin at the same time of nearly 4.5 million!), and boasted both a proud history and the fine architecture that so often goes with it. Its industries were many and varied; especially important were the metal work and small machinery, boilers, gasometers etc, although it was still perhaps better known for its foodstuffs (chocolates and preserves) and even better known as the leading centre of the book trade. In all, a strange and confusing choice of target with apparently little or no major military significance. But Harris and his planners clearly thought otherwise.

Take-off was at dusk, with the crew flying their first operation in A Wing and a Prayer and carrying their now 'standard' bomb load comprising two-thirds incendiaries to one third heavy explosive. Almost immediately after leaving Ludford, the Lancaster entered thick cloud, cloud that was to stay with them almost all the way to the target. Ted set to work early in jamming the GCI (Ground Control Intercept) instructions, with a running commentary from the Germans apparent shortly after take-off. The bomber stream comprised some 500 aircraft, nearly all Lancasters, and they were soon in trouble. Whilst the aircraft remained largely unmolested over the Dutch coast – a traditional happy hunting ground for the German nightfighter force – they were merely being lulled into a false sense of security. As they crossed the German frontier near Bremen, a tell-tale explosion in the sky denoted the first of 38 Lancasters that would be lost that night.

They reached Hannover unmolested until suddenly and terrifyingly their aircraft was coned by searchlights. Rusty threw A *Wing and a Prayer* into a violent weaving pattern, forcing the aircraft against its will into a series of steep banks and turns in a desperate bid to lose the fatal tentacle of light that could spell disaster.

Scores of other searchlights began seeking him out, hungry to capture him and hold him in their eerie yellow/blue shafts, such that wherever he went there was no escape. Rusty, blinded, his cockpit bathed in brilliant light frantically did everything in his power to throw the searchlights off the scent, before the heavy flak began to zero in on the target.

Somehow again fate was on their side. Rusty's violent manoeuvrings were enough to lose the beam, but he made sure by a series of further violent turns and dives such that he could return to the relative safety of the inky blackness around him. It was physically exhausting. Rusty made up the height he had lost by the time he reached the bombing run, giving Norman a clear sight of the target (or rather the TIs) from 22,000ft, largely undisturbed by the moderate heavy flak around them. Their cookie and multiple 4lb incendiaries safely despatched, Rusty headed for home taking a route out near Osnabrook, and was amongst the last to arrive at 22.55hrs after a six and a half hour flight.

It had been, in Rusty's words, a relatively quiet trip, and there was some hilarity at debriefing amongst the older hands when Rusty reported they had been 'attacked' by searchlights over Hannover. The joke was short-lived, however, for it had been a bad night for 101. Three crews were posted 'Missing': Flight Lieutenant Thomas Rowland, Pilot Officer Joseph

Slater and a 21 year-old Flight Sergeant Derek Bruce. The first two, in particular, were experienced crews that 101 could ill-afford to lose. Overall it had been a poor night for Bomber Command having lost 7.6 percent of its force including 11 Pathfinders; once again, 101 had also paid more than its fair share.

Another lull in the fighting meant more time for the crews to relax, and again there were a number of changes on the squadron including the departure of their CO, Wing Commander Carey Foster. He was posted away to Bomber Command headquarters, joining the Operational Staff at High Wycombe although his part in our story is not yet complete. In the meantime his place was taken on 18th January by Wing Commander R.I. 'Bob' Alexander, a regular officer who believed firmly in leading from the front.

Alexander was a 'second tour' man. He had already completed 33 operations with 216 and 108 Squadrons in Middle East Command, primarily flying Wellingtons. His courage was not in question; his 'press-on' approach may have endeared him to those of senior rank, and earn him a DFC, but met with a mixed response from those of more humble origins. Ted was to have personal experience of this later.

One of Alexander's first tasks was to sign the letters to the next-of-kin of those missing from operations on the 14th, including one to the wife of Flight Lieutenant Thomas Rowland (subsequently awarded a DFC), a 32 year-old former postman whom Alexander described as 'a most experienced and efficient pilot and Captain of his aircraft.' It was the first of many such letters he would have to write in the coming months.

'C' Flight also had a new commander with even more impressive credentials: Squadron Leader Charles Morton DFC

& Bar. Morton had won his first DFC as a young Pilot Officer in 1942. Flying with 12 Squadron to Wilhelmshafen on only his fourth operation, his aircraft was attacked by a Junkers 88 and badly shot about. Despite both gun turrets being out of action, his petrol tanks holed, and himself being wounded in the leg, Morton went on to bomb the target and return safely to base. He survived his first tour of operations, winning a second DFC in recognition of his 'exceptional fighting qualities' at a time when just to survive was exceptional. He would later go on to be awarded the Distinguished Service Order, the Station Commander describing him as having 'unflagging enthusiasm, dauntless determination, inspiring leadership and superb skill that few can emulate and none surpass.'

When the next Battle Order was posted – naming 20 crews for yet another attack on Berlin – Alexander's name was on it, flying as 'Second Dickey' with Morton – both flying their first operation since joining the Squadron.

Rusty's name, however, was not listed. His place had been taken by another novice crew, awaiting their first taste of battle. Ted was not so fortunate. Special Duties Operators were in short supply, and Ted found himself allocated – albeit temporarily he hoped – to a new crew in 'A' Flight, led by a Sergeant Sandford, a 22 year-old who, unusually for aircrew, had recently married. He had little or no time to get to know the others, the Flight Engineer Sergeant Smallman, Navigator Sergeant Barron, Wireless Operator Sergeant Simpson, Bomb Aimer Sergeant Ottewell, and the two gunners Sergeants Bartholemew and Alcock. All were desperately young, and in Ted's mind, desperately inexperienced. Ted felt uneasy from the start. He had his 'regular' crew. He knew them, trusted them. They had formed a bond, and knew that they could rely on one another to get them through. This crew was an unknown quantity. He was placing his life in their hands, and they nearly took it.

Take-off was at least uneventful. Ted could not see, already ensconced in his secret world, but outside a party of half a dozen or so ground-crew and support staff had lined up by the chequered control caravan to wave them off. As the Lancaster (DV 236 'G' George) cleared the perimeter fence and began to make height, already Ted was noticing a distinct lack of discipline in the air which instilled him with little confidence. He was happy to be away from it all, as blissfully unaware as it was possible to be of the chaotic way in which the crew performed. Ted tuned his equipment to the German Controllers' frequencies and began jamming, but no sooner had one blip appeared on his screen, then another was in evidence, and inevitably some of the commentary was getting through. Outside, the German nightfighters had begun to have a number of early successes, with each aircraft afire shining like a beacon to attract other nightfighters into the Bomber Stream. It was a major raid, involving some 769 aircraft, and despite taking a northerly route to throw the German off the scent, the controllers had not be fooled.

Also busy were the Pathfinders. Through their H2S sets (a navigational aid which displayed a graphical representation of the ground below) they had identified what they took to be the Eastern quarter of the City, but the target was inevitably obscured by heavy cloud, and they had to resort to the Wanganui method of marking the target. (Wanganui was the brainchild of Squadron Leader 'Artie' Ashworth DSO DFC AFC and named after his home town in New Zealand. The idea was simple: when the target was cloud covered, the Pathfinders marked with flares a point in the sky at which the Bombers should aim and in theory hit the 'invisible' target below. At first, Wanganui was greeted with incredulity but over time proved surprisingly effective.)

Each of the 101 Squadron aircraft bombed the Wanganui flares. Remarkably, in Ted's mind, the Sandford crew had made it through to the target area, dropping their bombs from 20,000ft at 19.52 hours and at a speed approaching 165 IAS. Through the clouds, the bomb aimer could make out a glow from fires in the target area, and the cloud base was illuminated by searchlights. The attack appeared concentrated and a column of smoke was seen rising to 23,000ft.

Sandford landed back at Ludford at one minute past midnight, joined in the circuit by an Australian, Flight Sergeant Kidd. Squadron Leader Morton – with the Wingco on board – had landed 10 minutes earlier. Ted was relieved. It had been a far from comfortable trip, and the novice crew had scared him half to death with their performance. Little did he know that the next night he would be doing it all over again.

Before the war, Magdeberg had been a beautiful city. As the capital of the Prussian province of Saxony, situated on the left bank of the Elbe, the City boasted a heritage dating back to the 9th Century, with narrow crooked streets and a magnificent cathedral, dedicated to SS Maurice and Catherine, a beautiful blend of the Romanesque and Gothic architecture. On the 21st January, the RAF, in its first major attack on that City in the war, did its utmost to raze it to the ground.

The target for the night, of course, was not the cathedral, nor any of the other historic buildings close by. The target, as the Intelligence Officer made clear at briefing, was the ironworks, in particular the Grusonwerke (part of Krupp), and the many other buildings and chemical industries on which the City thrived.

Ted was again crewed with Sandford, and if he thought the previous night had caused him to age prematurely, the events of that night were to confirm him as an octogenarian at 19! The nightfighters were in the stream before it crossed the German border, and whilst the German controller was reportedly slow to identify Magdeberg as the target (hardly surprising at it had never been subjected to a Main Force attack before), this did not stop the nightfighters from a number of early successes. In all, Bomber Command was to lose 57 aircraft that night – 35 Halifaxes and 22 Lancasters – a staggering 8.8% of the total force, and 15.6% of the total Halifax contingent. Lancaster DV 302 'H' Harry, flown by Sandford with Ted on board, was very nearly a victim itself.

Neither of the gunners, both only 19 years of age, saw the fighter that very nearly accounted for their lives. Too late they spotted the shadowy figure of the enemy aircraft as it manoeuvred itself into position for the kill. Miraculously, or perhaps because he was a novice himself, the German failed to take his chance. Ted felt rather than heard the unique sensation of canon and machine-gun fire tearing through the fuselage, fortunately failing to deliver the knock-out blow. The pilot began throwing the Lancaster around the night sky, recovering his composure, and height, climbing once again to bombing altitude of 21,000ft. The raid was not developing as planned. Many of the Main Force aircraft were already over the target as Sandford arrived; winds had been much stronger than forecast, and although H-hour had been set, 27 aircraft – mostly with H2S sets of their own – decided not to wait for the Pathfinder flares. Chaos might so easily have ensued. Many of the 15 aircraft aloft from 101 Squadron, led by the 'A' Flight commander Squadron Leader Marshall were reporting an absence of Pathfinder flares which resulted in at least one – an aircraft piloted by an Australian Flight Sergeant Irving –

bombing the flak and searchlights at Brunswick. The bomb aimer in Sandford's crew, Sergeant Ottewell, also could not see the target clearly, bombing instead the estimated position of the TI Greens seen 13 minutes before he dropped his own bombs! Around them the heavy flak grew more intense. The smell of cordite was very much in evidence, wafting through the fuselage of the already-damaged Lancaster until the German gunners found their range, and shrapnel began clattering against the airframe of the bomber, causing slight damage. Somewhere in the night an aircraft exploded. It may have been the one piloted by Flying Officer Perry, a Canadian, later listed as 'Missing' with his entire crew.

Ted again made it home, his fifth mission successfully completed, against the odds. He vowed never again to fly with what he would later describe as his 'nightmare' crew. He valued his life too highly, and was anxious to get back into the fold of the crew he had begun to see as his own family (and who at that time were down the local celebrating Rusty's 21st birthday). But before he could, one more trial was yet to befall him, and the fate of the Sandford crew would be sealed for eternity.

No-one at the time knew exactly what happened to Austin 'Sandy' Sandford. As the phrase in the Squadron Operations Record Book would record with monotonous regularity, no communications had been received since take-off. In fact, his aircraft had been hit by flak, and the crippled aircraft finished off by a nightfighter, crashing near the town of Northeim. His was one of 33 Lancasters lost on the night of 27th/28th January on a heavy raid to Berlin to which 101 had committed 16 aircraft including both the 'A' and 'C' Flight Commanders. Sandford had taken his regular crew with him, with the exception of the navigator. Having the misfortune of being the replacement navigator that evening was Flying Officer John Clarke, 24, who died with six of the others; the eighth man in the crew, the Flight Engineer, escaped to become a POW (and was co-incidentally re-patriated on 6th February 1945 on the same ship as John Jossa).

Ted had found himself on the Battle Order to fly with Flying Officer Goeres, a very earnest and serious-minded Canadian in 'B' Flight. They had a relatively quiet trip. Finding the target obscured by cloud, like most Bomber Command aircraft that evening they bombed the Wanganui flares. Goeres didn't hang around. Ted liked that. Just like Rusty, as soon as he had bombed and the photo had been taken, Goeres put the nose down slightly to gain speed and pulled his finger out for the long journey home. The route out to the target had taken them a little over three hours, but the winds that had carried them there so swiftly were now making the return leg inexorably long. Goeres, Lancaster DV 264 'L' and crew landed back at Ludford at 02.20, nearly nine hours after they had left.

In the interrogation that followed, it appeared that despite the need for sky markers, they had 'pranged' the target well. Warrant Officer (soon to be Pilot Officer) Laurens, a South African-born pilot who had been awarded the Distinguished Flying Medal for 'conspicuous courage' after only his 11th operation, had told the Intelligence Officer 15 minutes earlier that they had seen a concentration of fires visible at a distance of some 160 miles. Flight Sergeant 'Dutch' Holland, an Australian in a near-all-Australian crew had similarly reported well concentrated fires. Post-raid analysis by the Germans revealed that a number of industrial premises had indeed been hit, and several important war industries had suffered a serious setback. In all it had been a good night's work. A long night. But at least Ted was alive.

January was proving to be a busy month for 101 Squadron. Whenever Bomber Command flew, 101 had Squadron aircraft in the air. It was a proud tradition, but it often cost them dearly. Throughout January, the Squadron flew on all eight of Bomber Command's raids, a total of 110 sorties. Its targets were Stettin, Magdeberg, Brunswick, and Berlin – the latter five times. It had lost something in the order of 60 men, two for each day of the month, with several more 'missing'.

There was no let-up. Harris, no doubt frustrated at almost two weeks of inactivity at the start of the month, now ordered an increase in tempo. It was unrelenting. On the $28^{th}/29^{th}$ and again on $30^{th}/31^{st}$, 101 contributed 29 aircraft and crews out of a total Command Force over the two attacks of more than 1200 bombers.

Alexander joined the Squadron for the first of the attacks, but was frustrated by an early return. It would not put the Wing Commander in a good mood. It was his first solo trip with the Squadron, and he was eager to lead from the front. The remaining 13 crews took a long route over Northern Denmark, a challenge for the navigators without the benefit of H2S (101 Squadron aircraft could not take the weight of the SDO, his ABC technology and H2S as well) but deemed wholly necessary to keep out of range of the German night-fighters. But some of them got through.

"Dive, starboard!"

One of the gunners had shouted on the intercom. Tommy or Harry once again on the qui vive and once again proving their greatest defence was their vigilance. Rusty turned and ruddered the Lancaster to starboard, skidding the bomber slightly to throw the German off his aim. It was another Ju 88, a 300 mph fighter armed with three 20mm cannon and three

7.9mm machine guns in the nose, and Liechtenstein radar. The German pilot was good, and determined.

"He's coming at us again. When I give the word dive, dive port. Dive, dive, dive!"

Again Rusty rolled the heavy bomber, this time in the opposite direction in a desperate attempt to lose the enemy aircraft. And yet still it came. The physical exertion of having to weave the mighty Lancaster across the night sky was beginning to tell. Rusty needed all his strength and flying skill to corkscrew the aircraft one more time.

"That did it," said one of the others. "We've lost him."

Rusty asked the crew to report any damage. *A Wing and a Prayer* had been hit. One of the attacks had accounted for the mid-upper escape hatch which had been blown out. The icy wind was now whistling down the length of the fuselage, making life uncomfortable for everyone, especially Tommy in the mid-upper turret and Ted almost directly below it. Even Taffy in his 'warm spot', was regretting for once his decision not to wear his fleece-lined flying boots.

After all the excitement, Rusty began climbing, on instruction from Alec who had already given him a course to steer after the violent manoeuvrings. Take off had been midnight, and by the time they arrived over Berlin, shortly after 03.00, the attack was already in full swing and appeared to be well concentrated. Norman was once again in his element, but disappointed at yet again not being able to see any ground-markers, and having to resort to Wanganui (still, they were just as colourful!). As he prepared the computer and set the bomb-release sequence, he saw a massive explosion in the target area and made a record of the time. It was 03.20.

Elsewhere, others within 101 were having a busy night. Warrant Officer Johnny Batten-Smith, a young and likeable pilot who was later to die in tragic circumstances over Nuremberg, had managed to find an extra few hundred feet in height. His bomb aimer, Flight Sergeant Ross, noted a huge explosion just after they had dropped their own 4000lb 'cookie' and mixed incendiaries which lasted for a whole minute, and large areas completely covered by fires.

Flying Officer Todd, a New Zealander flying in 'H', saw the same explosion and two subsequent explosions three minutes apart. The bombs were finding their targets. The new Chancellery, the State Patent Office, and a number of theatres, hospitals and embassies had been hit, and nearly 200,000 Berliners displaced.

By now however, the German nightfighters were also finding their targets. 'Blips' were appearing regularly on Ted's oscilloscope as he fiddled with the dials and pressed the switch that would hopefully drown out the controller's instructions with its strange warbling. Some 46 aircraft would be lost that night; A *Wing and a Prayer* was already riding her luck.

"Bandits, Bandits, single fighter attacking. Range approximately 2000 yards. Prepare to corkscrew port. Corkscrew port. Go!"

The gunners had again seen an FW 190 trying to catch them unawares, and for the fourth time that night, Rusty put the aircraft into a diving turn to port just as the fighter opened fire and his own gunners responded, the barrels of their browning machine guns now burning hot, the empty .303 cartridge cases disappearing into the night sky. As soon as it appeared, so the fighter vanished again into the cloud.

"That was bloody close," someone said and they all thought. The operation was proving to be a marathon of endurance. Behind them, 150 miles away, the glow from the fires over the target could still be seen. They were all tired, but a combination of adrenaline and the 'Wakey-Wakey' tablets issued to all aircrew were keeping them alert. And a good thing too, because before the night was over they were attacked for a fifth time by an unidentified aircraft that made a single pass and disappeared, beaten off by the gunners.

Despite all the unwanted aerobatics and the loss in height and course, Alec's navigation was still spot on. Alec asked Norman for a pin point.

"I can't see anything but we're right on track!" he joked. Norman knew, as did the others, that Alec's navigation was virtually without equal.

They crossed the English coast at their expected landfall, just as the sun was coming up for another day, and joined the circuit over Ludford at 08.15 – one of the first to arrive back.

As the engines were switched off, and the crew prepared to disembark, Rusty noticed a small hole on the port side level with his head. On the starboard side, was a corresponding hole. At some stage during one of the attacks, a cannon shell or splinter had passed right through the cockpit and exited the other side, and should by rights have passed through Rusty's body on its way. He must have been leaning forward. The caul that his father had given him for luck, that had seen him safely through the First World War and that his son now carried in a little tobacco tin in his Battledress pocket, had worked a miracle.

The next day they did it all over again.

Jock had affected all of the necessary repairs, and they were in the air by 17.15. This time however, they managed to avoid most of the excitement that they had witnessed the previous evening. They experienced some icing in the cloud, and in the bright moonlight, A Wing and a Prayer found itself in formation with another 101 Squadron Lancaster, SR I flown by Pilot Officer Philip Rowe, and another Lancaster from an Australian Squadron, No 467. Fighter flares dropped by

Luftwaffe aircraft to signal the presence of the Bomber Stream were much in evidence, but apart from a brief sighting of a Ju 88 over the target area (which fortunately didn't see them), the trip was largely uneventful.

The bombs were dropped on time, on target, and a large red explosion reported in the target area. In less than seven hours after leaving Ludford, the crew had finished their interrogation and were enjoying their post-op bacon and eggs. One 'C' Flight aircraft was missing. Flight Sergeant Douglas Froggatt and crew would not be returning – a victim of a nightfighter attack – although three would survive as POWs.

For the next few days, Ted enjoyed a short spell of leave. The Squadron and indeed the whole of Bomber Command did little or no flying during this time, and with the exception of a specialist raid by 617 Squadron on the Gnome & Rhone aero engine factory in Limoges on the 8th/9th February there were no operations. That's not to say there still wasn't a great deal to be done about the station. The lull gave crews an opportunity to hone various skills, gunnery tests, practice bombing, fighter affiliation, dingy drills. Curly in particular used the time with Jock and the lads working on 'W' at dispersal; some of the others went too, believing they were being helpful but probably just getting in the way. Norman spent much of his spare time in the Link Trainer – a very early flight simulator – where he would practice instrument flying, maintaining air speed, height and navigational flying until he became rather proficient, even learning the beam approach system. He did this for two reasons: firstly out of love for the sensation of flying; and secondly because if anything happened to Rusty, he figured one of them at least should have some idea of how to fly a plane!

During any Stand Down period, everybody took the opportunity to get away from the base, even if it was for just a few hours. Ted disappeared with Alec to a local farmhouse where they could get eggs and fried bread. Norman – if not practice 'flying' – took his washing to a lady he'd come across in the village and who laundered his clothes to his satisfaction. (Norman was very particular about his appearance; in the absence of modern-day facilities, he used to place his trousers under the mattress and sleep on them so that when he woke up they had a perfect crease). Tommy spent precious time with his wife who was now heavily pregnant (the crew would later club together to buy the new-born a pram). Taffy found somewhere – anywhere – where he could spend his basic pay (and sixpence a day danger money for flying over Germany) on drink.

During this period, the Squadron also had a visit from the press, the first of several such visits in the coming months. This was the first visit by the respected journalist Carl Olsson from Illustrated magazine, accompanied by his photographer R. Saidman. Olsson had already built up a good knowledge of the workings of a bomber squadron, but remarked on the tremendous changes that were evident since his last feature 12 months before. In his article 'Good-bye Berlin', published on February 19th (Olsson was to write a similar follow-up feature the following month), he wrote:

"Gone are the days of central heating and the comfortable, brick-built living quarters of the so-called permanent stations. With few exceptions these have now been put to other purposes. And the RAF has been very generous in handing over its best accommodation to our American and other Allies.

"Officers and men live alike in the same kind of Nissen huts dumped down on communal sites, often with no such thing as 'water laid on' and with a mile and more of unmade roads separating them from their messes and their working quarters.

"The nearest town with a couple of pubs and one picture palace is often several miles away, and RAF regulations – harder on petrol restrictions than most civilian authorities, allow no free transport to get there. Station entertainment is limited to a cinema projector. ENSA shows are unknown because there is no timber to build a stage. It is a front-line existence almost as completely as if they were operating from a newly conquered territory.

"But if they grumble a bit (and who wouldn't?) they grumble cheerfully and give their stations nicknames usually based on the word mud. And they carry on working even harder than the RAF has ever done before in its history.

"This station I visited, for instance, only came into being last July. The bombers flew in, and air and ground crews arrived long before the constructors' men were off the site. The aircrews were over Germany the day after their arrival at the new station. Since that day they have taken several thousand tons of bombs to Germany – most of them to Berlin."

While Olsson took the notes for his article and spoke to the men, the cameraman took a variety of shots to 'capture' squadron life: a Lancaster lined up for take-off, waiting for a 'green' from the Flying Control caravan; aircrew rations being checked and packed; lines of shoes in the cloakroom, contrasted against a similar shot of mud-caked gumboots (which would feature with the caption: ' a picture that tells its own story'); the crew of 'K' King about to board their aircraft; a mighty cookie. Saidman also had Rusty, Harry and Alec amongst others grouped around the tea urn, filling their thermos flasks supposedly before an operation. Everyone took part willingly, and it proved a pleasant distraction, breaking the monotony from their usual humdrum existence.

Olsson added: "Multiply the weight of attack achieved by this station by the many scores of similar stations in the command and one begins to realise why the great city of Hamburg has vanished from the lists of the world ports, and why Berlin is being erased as the centre of the German war machine."

Berlin was indeed being erased, and Harris' obsession with the target was far from being abated. When at last the weather cleared sufficiently over England and the Continent to resume operations, it was no surprise that the choice of target would again be the Nazi capital. And as if to make a point of his frustration, Harris ordered the largest force yet to attack the city – nearly 900 aircraft – including more than 500 Lancasters.

The Waughman crew had another relatively quiet trip. It seemed to be a strange quirk in their operational tour both previously and in what was to come that they had trips where nothing happened one minute, and then the next they were lucky to make it back. It was another afternoon take-off, and 101 Squadron put up 22 crews, including the Wing Commander. Perhaps it was luck, or perhaps the result of the elaborate diversions and a long route north over Denmark but what they did see seemed to be happening to other people. The target area was covered in fighter flares which spelled trouble, and they were right to be on their guard. The German Controller had in fact ordered the fighters not to fly over Berlin, leaving the area free from the Flak, but the flares were evidence that many of the fighters were ignoring their orders, and attacking the bombers over the City. It was the hottest yet, and despite the cloud, the glow of fires were visible 80-100 miles after leaving the target. For once Norman had been able to bomb ground markers, and at interrogation, most of the Captains reported a successful op. Only Pilot Officer McConnell DFC was missing, on a night where the German defences had brought down some 43 aircraft. McConnell and the two gunners perished; the remainder, including the SDO Pilot Officer Fischl, were taken prisoner.

The operation on the 15th February proved to be the end of what could be thought of as the 'true' Battle of Berlin, especially for Rusty. Ted and the others, however, would fly one more trip to Berlin with a different skipper, but over the course of the next few weeks the order of the day was variety. It was as though Harris had sought out his atlas of Germany and decided to systematically raid any City of his fancy: Stuttgart, Frankfurt, Essen, Nuremberg, Cologne. None were on the 'official' Pointblank Directive to smash aircraft production and its supporting industries. All, in his mind and the mind of his planning staff, however, had sound strategic value. On the 19th, the briefing room map showed the red ribbon extending deep into enemy territory, to the City of Leipzig, a beautiful old City of narrow streets and numerous 16th and 17th Century houses with high-pitched roofs. Amongst its churches was the Thomas Kirche, where J Sebastian Bach had once been the organist. It was considered the third city after Berlin and Hamburg for trade, but it was for its importance in aircraft production and as a railway centre that made it such an essential target. Leipzig, throughout history, had been no stranger to conflict, and in the 30 Years War suffered six sieges and was occupied four times. It was about to be laid siege again, this time in the form of more than 800 Lancasters, Halifaxes and Mosquitoes from the RAF.

Bomber Command was about to suffer its greatest loss up to that point in the war. But again, bizarrely, A *Wing and a Prayer* and her crew were to come through completely unscathed. At briefing, there were the usual whistles and catcalls as the target was announced, but also more than a few raised eyebrows. Leipzig was an unusual target. It had only been raided twice previously, the last time in December 1943. But that was a lifetime ago. No-one could remember it, although the Squadron did lose an aircraft piloted by Flight Lieutenant Frazer-Hollins. It was another maximum effort, and 101 put up 21 aircraft for the night's operations. The Wing Commander was in an especially ebullient mood as he would be going with them – Alexander never shied away from an operation, although Squadron Commanders with his experience were by no means forced into operations. Indeed they were considered too valuable to lose, and some had to be ordered to stop flying.

The Intelligence Officer and various Section Leaders ran through what they knew. Stirlings, long-since withdrawn from the Main Force because of their unacceptably high casualty rate, would fly a diversionary minelaying sortie to Kiel; Mosquitoes would also fly a diversion to Berlin giving the locals another interrupted night's sleep and continuing the war of nerves. Halifaxes in the Stream were always welcomed by the Lancaster boys, since their performance meant they seemed to attract a disproportionate amount of attention from the flak and fighters. The route to target was detailed, crossing the Dutch coast, avoiding the worst of the Ruhr defences and then the long leg to the target. It was not an elaborate route; the diversions should keep most of the German nightfighter force at bay.

There was a great deal of discussion after the briefing as the crews attempted to while away the time until take off, which had been set for 11-30. It was going to be a long haul – more than 1000 miles there and back, perhaps seven or eight hours – deep into occupied territory. They knew what to expect with Berlin, but Leipzig was an unknown quantity. It was bound to be a bit dicey.

Rusty started his take-off run at 23.44. The significant fuel-load and unhelpful weather conditions meant for once Norman was not in the nose for take-off. Rusty wouldn't allow it. As the heavy bomber lumbered along the runway, slowly building up speed, Rusty called to Curly:

"Through the gate."

Curly concurred, pushing all four throttle levers forward beyond the maximum into emergency boost to gain the extra power needed for take-off. The mighty bomber shuddered and roared in protest, shaking the airframe and the men inside her to the very core. Norman's heart was in his mouth. Then, suddenly, they were airborne as Rusty lifted the Lancaster over the boundary wire, bringing the undercarriage up as he did so.

Reaching the assembly point, the crew settled down for the long trip to the target. Throttles had been eased back. Over the North Sea, when it was deemed safe to do so, Harry, Tommy and Norman asked permission to test their guns. The faint smell of cordite could be sensed as they did so. Ted was already busy. Taffy had received a signal from HQ with a number of frequencies to scan, and already the German Controllers knew the force was on its way, and had not been totally fooled by the diversions. Only a small part of the fighter force had been sent to investigate the attack on Kiel, leaving the majority of fighters ready to intercept the Main Force as it crossed the Dutch Coast. Battle was soon joined. An exploding aircraft to starboard, and the appearance of the first of a number of fighter flares signalled danger.

Alec was growing concerned. Taffy listened in for the Group broadcasts that came every 10 minutes past and 20 minutes to the hour. Other aircraft in the Stream were tasked with signalling HQ with any changes in weather conditions that were in turn communicated to the rest of the Group.

This helped Alec with navigation, but according to his calculations, their ETA was going to cause problems. He called Rusty:

"We'll have to lose a bit of time skipper, or we'll be too early on target," Alec said.

"How much time Navigator?"

"About 20 minutes. The wind must have changed. We'll have to reduce speed and dog-leg. I'll give you a course to steer."

"OK Alec. When you're ready."

Rusty had unquestionable faith in his Navigator. If Alec said they would be 20 minutes too early over the target, then he knew best. The danger of being over the target before the allotted bombing time (H-Hour) were obvious. The Pathfinders wouldn't be there, which meant there would be no marking and nothing to aim at. No-one wanted to stooge around the target area waiting for the Pathfinders to show, however, so it was better to try and lose time now, rather than circle around Leipzig advertising your presence to all and sundry and inviting the Germans to come and have a go at you.

Rusty continued the dog-leg, throttling back but maintaining height at a little over 23,000ft. A *Wing and a Prayer* was performing well. He was glad to have the extra height. The searchlights that were probing the night skies were proving largely ineffectual, but the fighter flares were now so abundant that night was turning rapidly into day. Another bomber exploded in the distance, the victim of a direct hit. It was obvious to all of them now that the night was not going well. Hundreds of other bombers had arrived in the target area too early and were now orbiting, waiting for the Pathfinders to arrive. Like Tuna caught in an ever shrinking net, the bombers began to be picked off one by one. Another huge explosion nearby, unlike anything they had seen before as two aircraft collided. Flak was now also beginning to find its mark, although the shell bursts at 23,000ft were only largely light. 10/10ths cloud obscured the target as at last the first of the Wanganui flares began to go down shortly after 04.00. A red glow could be seen through the clouds as Norman waited for his moment to drop the bombs. Bombs gone and photo taken, Rusty opened the throttles to take them out of the target area as quickly as possible while Alec called the new course to steer.

It was a relief to get back within sight of home as Rusty called Flying Control for permission to land. One other aircraft was in the circuit, flown by Warrant Officer Evans. As he cleared the runway, Rusty was called to Pancake. It was 06.55.

There was a great deal of excitement and consternation at debriefing. Most of the crews were reporting exploding aircraft, a few were moaning about the late arrival of the Pathfinders and how the Met forecast could have been so wrong. The Met Officer had some explaining to do. It was clear that the losses for the night would be considerable, but as the new day dawned only one aircraft from 101 Squadron was missing, that flown by Pilot Officer John Laurens DFM, the young South African who had been to Berlin on no fewer than seven occasions and was by then considerably advanced in his tour. It would subsequently transpire that Laurens, his Wireless Op Pilot Officer Cassian Waight and one other crew member, Sergeant William Bolt, had all been killed, shot down near Groningen, Holland. Five survived the crash to be interned for the rest of the war.

Overall, however, 101 Squadron had escaped lightly. As the picture emerged of an apparently successful raid, at least in part, the losses began to reach a disturbingly high total. Some

76 bombers were missing – 9.5% of the force. The Halifax losses, as a percentage of the total force despatched, was far higher.

Leipzig was a big defeat. Had it not been for a far greater disaster at Nuremberg six weeks later, it might have been given more attention in history as one of the low points in Bomber Command's history. Like so many things in war, however, the disaster was more down to bad luck than planning. Every measure had been taken to deceive the German nightfighters, but Harris' greatest enemy, the weather, had perhaps played the biggest part in the losses that night. Four aircraft were lost in collisions over the target area, and at least 20 were shot down by flak. Common sense, and a comparison with the Mailly-Le-Camp raid in May 1944 (of which more later), suggest that to hang around a target area waiting to bomb was lethal. Bomber Command had to learn its lesson. One positive outcome from the disaster was the withdrawal of the Halifax IIs and Halifax Vs from doing any further operations over Germany. Only its more powerful successor, the Halifax III with its Bristol Hercules engines, would now be allowed to share front-line responsibility with the Lancaster.

The next night they went to Stuttgart, as Rusty noted in his diary "Southern Germany for a change". They didn't see much on the way to the target, save for a little heavy flak, and for once could see the town through the clouds from a height of 23,500ft as well as a couple of very large explosions as their own load of cookies and incendiaries added to the mayhem. Stuttgart was as successful as Leipzig was a disaster. Only nine aircraft were lost, although another five were lost in crashes over England. It was another long haul, nearly eight hours, landing at 07.32.

The raid on Stuttgart was significant for other reasons; it was the last time that Rusty flew as a non-commissioned Officer. During the lull in fighting in early February, Rusty had been recommended for a Commission. Many aircraft Captains who were deemed to demonstrate the right calibre regardless of their educational or social backgrounds, were offered Commissions. The Class system, which had predominated in the early war years to determine who should be officers and who should remain as NCOs had largely disappeared, primarily through necessity. Many were dead. In some respects it exemplified the law of diminishing returns, that ultimately the pool from which officers had been traditionally fished had dried up.

Rusty's commissioning came about without any preliminary board of assessment. He was simply called into the CO's office, congratulated, and handed a voucher for £90 and a travel warrant to London, and advised to go to Burberry's to get his uniform. He returned, with a pristine uniform and the half ring of a Pilot Officer, a proud man. But it didn't last long. Later, the eight of them set off for the White Hart to celebrate, and Taffy did his utmost to ensure his 'new' skipper didn't get ideas above his station. In keeping with tradition, he pinched Rusty's new peaked cap, filled it with beer, and proceeded to drink the contents as it spilled from the vent holes in the side. Rusty returned to camp with a sore head, and crumpled uniform, suitably 'commissioned'.

Rusty's new status had some practical implications, notably that he had to leave the Sergeants Mess and billet with the officers. He was sorry to leave There was little difference between the officers' and the sergeants' billets. He had a locker and a rug by the side of the bed, as well as a bedside table and better curtains at the window. The main advantage, as far as Rusty could see, was that he had his bed made, and shoes and best blue uniform cleaned by a batwoman who looked after the hut. The main disadvantage was one of morale. Not only was Rusty separated from his own crew and them from him, but he was now sharing with officers from a variety of different crews, which meant the chances of at least somebody going missing form the hut on ops was greatly increased. Anyone could be affected. Two in the hut, for example, both second tour men with more than 50 ops under their belts failed to return one night.

Whilst Rusty was engaged climbing the ranks, Ted was required for another operation with yet another different pilot, Flying Officer McKenna. Ted had not originally been on the Battle Order. The regular SDO with the McKenna crew in V-Victor was a Pilot Officer Scott, but at the last minute a replacement was sought, and Ted found himself in the wrong place at the wrong time. McKenna was an experienced New Zealander, and the trip, to Schweinfurt, was uneventful. It was a major raid or 734 aircraft, designed to finish the job started by the Americans in daylight the previous day (it was now February 24th).

The raid was significant in that Harris divided his force into two, and set their bombing times two hours apart. Many of the German nightfighters, deceived by earlier diversions, therefore found themselves on the ground at the critical moment, and only 22 aircraft were lost in the first wave and a further 11 in the second. Alexander, who was flying himself that night, was not pleased about the early returns – there were three, but all of the crews that made it through to the target reported seeing a large concentration of fires and several large explosions through the smoke and the haze. It was a long trip – eight and three-quarter hours – landing back at base at 05.00. All of the Squadron's aircraft returned safely.

For almost two weeks at the end of February/start of March, it snowed. It snowed like it can only snow in Lincolnshire, thick white dunes impassable to man or beast. Snow three feet deep with drifts up to 16ft. It was also bitterly cold, which made life for the air and ground crews at Ludford almost intolerable. The Nissen huts in which they slept were unlined, and prone to condensation. This used to run down the corrugations of the sheeting from which the huts were constructed and invariably freeze. There was heating, in the form of a pot stove. This was about 250mm in diameter and about a meter high. There was a circular lid they could lift off to stoke the fire, and a flap at the bottom to remove the ashes. A chimney pipe extended from the top upwards out through the roof. Coal was the main fuel, although this was rationed. Occasionally they would augment their own supply by mounting a raid on a neighbouring hut. Failing that, the odd chair or table would disappear. Keeping warm became fundamental to life. Each night, presuming they had enough fuel, they would stoke the fire until it glowed white hot in the hope that when they woke up in the morning, it would still be warm. Taffy took to moving his bedstead as close to the stove as possible. Each morning he would spit at it; if it sizzled, he got up. If it didn't, he wrapped himself up tighter and stayed in bed.

The snow meant little or no flying. Harris was being robbed of his chance to consistently smash the industry, buildings, homes and morale of the German people. To the men at Ludford Magna, the snow meant an opportunity of regressing back to their childhood with some of the best snowball fights they had ever had against rival huts, and the hilarious sight of Taffy rolling in the snow naked! It was a toss-up of what was less welcome – the snow or the mud. For four days solid, between 1st and 4th March, any of the crews not flying were

97

engaged in snow clearing. The whole gang turned out, suitably clothed in Sheepskins and woolly hats with spades and shovels to try and keep the aerodrome operational. Six crews (including Flying Officer Goeres and Johnny Batten-Smith) flew to an advance base at Wickenby and operated from there, raiding Stuttgart on the night of $1^{st}/2^{nd}$. Some local flying was also possible – air tests and fighter affiliation for example, and on the 10th Rusty flew down to West Raynham and back with Flight Lieutenant Dickinson, the 'C' Flight deputy commander.

Wing Commander Alexander was impressed with the commitment shown by his men. On 5th March he wrote:

> "During the recent state of emergency, special efforts were called for from all ranks. The response to that call was immediate and the special effort was forthcoming with a spirit which was a subject for admiration. We were able, thanks to your loyalty, to operate six aircraft against Germany on the night of 1st March. That may appear small in number, but it was vital that we should operate and the work required to get those aircraft off called for a maximum effort from all ranks. To me it means more than the fact that six aircraft took off from this airfield. The routine and organisation required to operate under normal conditions calls for effort enough, but the true test of a squadron is made when they are required to increase that effort to combat emergency conditions. You were tested, and did not fail."

He added with a flourish:

> "I am indeed proud to serve with you. Thank you."

By now, Ted had gained valuable operational experience. Schweinfurt was his 12th operation, and there were figures, proven figures, that said your chances of surviving a tour of operations after 12 trips increased dramatically. Ops 13 and 14 were both tough targets – Stuttgart (again) and Frankfurt. Back with Rusty, on both occasions they came through unscathed. Stuttgart on 15th, was a fairly quiet trip. Rusty had to dog-leg to lose time (adverse weather conditions again) and when he got there the Pathfinders were nine minutes late over the target. When they finally arrived, the marking was excellent, and Rusty would note in his diary that evening "Fairly long but a better prang than last time." Over Frankfurt on 18th March, for once most of the way was free from cloud but over the target they were not so lucky. Thick 10/10ths layers obscured everything. They saw nothing save a number of large well concentrated fires, and returned after a relatively short trip of six hours.

The Squadron lost two crews: those of Pilot Officer James Clegg over Stuttgart, and Pilot Officer Roy Dixon returning from Frankfurt. Both were Squadron characters. James Clegg, a 29 year-old Manxman from Peel, was a George Medal holder. Roy Dixon, who had come up through the ranks and only recently been commissioned, had won a Distinguished Flying Medal aged 20 on his first operation, beating off sustained attacks from flak and fighters. Dixon had been dreadfully unlucky. His aircraft had suffered a total engine failure and crashed in Norfolk on the homeward leg, killing all on board. It was poor reward for his earlier heroism.

No sooner had Ted re-acquainted himself with his 'regular' skipper that he was again picked to fly with a different pilot. There was some consternation when he learned who. On the Battle Order he saw the familiar names of Ormerod, Cowan, Arndell, Westby, Dewsbury and Nunn. Under Aircraft Captain he read the name Alexander. The Wing Commander himself. Alexander had taken to captaining a number of different crews on operations, and indeed was well-known for his willingness to fly with any crew, regardless of their experience, in the understandable belief that it was good for Squadron morale. Ted didn't feel that his morale needed a boost especially, and neither did the others, but they had little choice in the matter.

Dutifully the crews began to converge at the briefing room. It was early afternoon. They took their places at the trestle tables and stood around smoking and chatting, waiting for the arrival of the 'brass'. A shout of 'Attention!' at the back, and they stood stiffly, shoulders squared, hands down at their sides as the senior station personnel entered in strict order of rank, Group Captain King in the lead. The Military Policeman at the rear closed the door behind him, and stood guard outside.

With the roll-call duly completed, the Senior IO drew forward, pointing to the map on the wall and uttering the words he had last spoken more than a month before:

"Your target for tonight Gentlemen is the Big City, Berlin…"

Old hands feigned indifference. Most had guessed anyway. Full petrol loads, a 2000 pounder, 36 x 30lbs bombs and hundreds of incendiaries narrowed the options down to a few. They hadn't been to Berlin for so long that it seemed a likely prospect they would be going tonight. Newer crews listened intently, bewildered at their new surroundings as the IO completed his customary briefing on the importance of the target to the German War machine, and more importantly, the increased night fighter strength and any known positions of flak and searchlights. It was going to be a big raid, a maximum effort, 811 aircraft in all. This didn't mean that all 811 would get through and bomb the target. In most major raids in recent weeks, 50 and sometimes upwards of 100 aircraft failed to attack their target, either shot down, missing or an early return. On the last raid on Berlin on the night of the 15th/16th February, 891 bombers were despatched but only 806 successfully completed their operation. A total of 85 aircraft did not get through; 43 were missing.

The Met. forecast for the route and the target area, delivered by the Met Officer, looked encouraging for once. Although there would be strato-cumulus with tops of up to 5,000ft over much of the North Sea, this should become more scattered near the Danish coast with a real chance of clear skies over Berlin. Norman smiled to himself. It would make a change to be able to see the target properly. Then the Met Officer spoiled it by his usual caveat that of course the target could be totally obscured by cloud, it was always difficult to predict. Oh well, clear skies made it easier for searchlights, fighters and flak, so maybe clouds were better.

Pathfinder tactics for the evening would be 'Newhaven' (a blind marking technique using H2S) plus 'Wanganui', depending on conditions when they got there. The other leaders stood and gave their piece. Harry and Tommy, fast becoming experienced in their art and having already come across their fair share of enemy aircraft attacks, listened as Flight Lieutenant Hill, the Gunnery Leader talked about constant vigilance, not just looking at the aircraft attacking but also searching for the one you couldn't see. It was the usual routine but wise to listen for any new information of value.

Soon the briefing was over, pockets emptied, parachutes and survival packs collected, and then the interminable wait until take-off which had been set for 18.25. If they didn't have their regular pilot at least there was some satisfaction that the crew had their regular aircraft. Take-off was uneventful. Alexander had his own style, no-one would criticise a man for that, and it would be later in the flight that one or two of his idiosyncrasies would begin to get on the crew's nerves, and especially upset Curly.

From the coast of England to the rendezvous point, the Lancaster climbed through the low cloud into clear air, with the moon shining brightly and the stars brilliant overhead. Later, if there was time, Alec might get a chance for an astrofix, to check his calculations by more 'traditional' means. It was always good practice, and without the benefit of H2S to give him an accurate ground picture, often essential. The aircraft continued climbing, levelling off at 15,000ft. The gunners kept a good lookout; the Germans would know they were on their way by now, but at this stage Harry and Tommy were more keeping an eye out for other Lancasters or Halifaxes getting too close for comfort. With the wind on the port beam blowing strongly from the North, they were already drifting off track. The wind speeds they had been told to expect were dramatically wrong.

The aircraft lumbered on into the night, leaving the rendezvous point and pressing on the first major leg of its journey to the coast of Denmark. The wind forecast had mentioned a strong north-westerly up to 60 miles and hour. With their first landfall, Alec estimated the speed to be much more than this, possibly twice as strong. They didn't know it yet, but already a good many bombers were now drifting dangerously off track. If this continued, instead of making the correct landfall at the island of Romo, they would find themselves below the Sylt heading for the heavily-defended area between Flensburg and Kiel.

Alec was now becoming increasingly troubled. If his calculations were correct, and he had no reason to doubt them, the strength of the wind outside was now making them race to the target right at the front of the stream, and they were in danger of overtaking the Pathfinders. It was a repeat of the raid on

Leipzig, only this time the winds were much much faster. It was also freezing – in Harry's case quite literally. In the rear turret, the perspex had been cut away to allow greater visibility. The flip side was that Harry had little protection in real terms against temperatures which on a night like this and at height of 20,000ft could reach -40 degrees centigrade!

Elsewhere, the stream was becoming scattered, and the first bombers were already becoming victims to flak and fighters over the German/Danish border. Taffy began receiving wireless reports from Group about the possible error in wind speeds by a margin of 30 miles an hour. He passed the information through the curtain on tiny slips of paper to Alec which confirmed his own thoughts, although he still felt the winds were stronger still. There was another broadcast, which Taffy did not receive, to announce that the timing of the attack would now begin five minutes earlier.

Things were going rapidly wrong. By now they had reached their turning point north of Rostock. The leading wave was now well ahead of the planned H-Hour and well ahead of the arrival of the Pathfinders. Alec reported to the Captain.

"Navigator to Pilot. Skipper, we'll need to reduce speed, lose some time, otherwise we'll be too early on target."

"OK navigator, how much time do we have to lose?"

"About 10 minutes, the wind's a lot stronger than forecast."

As they spoke, flak began to appear in the distance and searchlights began probing the sky. Those navigators who didn't know how far south they had been pushed were in for a rude awakening, and conditions began to hot up still further as the first fighter flares began drifting down from above.

The minutes ticked by. Still they were going too fast. It was too late to dog-leg. There wasn't time. Alec suggested the only course open to them:

"You'll have to put your flaps down and drop your under-carriage Skipper. We're still going too fast. And you'll have to fly a circuit."

Alec was thinking on his feet. There simply wasn't time for a dog-leg so he chose the only option open to them. A 360 degree circuit was potentially hazardous, but Alec believed there was more danger still in arriving at the target before the markers had gone down.

Alexander did as instructed. To the absolute horror of the remaining crew, he lowered the aircraft's flaps and undercarriage until they were just above stalling speed. He then let the minutes tick by until they were due to bomb by approaching the target area at a speed a little above 120 knots! All except Alec thought Alexander was bloody stupid and he was scaring the hell out of them. Rusty always gained a little height so they could come in and bomb at speed, but the CO seemed to have gone stark staring bonkers and completely oblivious to either his crew's feelings, or the merry hell that was going on outside.

Ahead of them, chaos reigned. Despite desperate attempts by Group to amend the plan 'on the hoof', several aircraft had already bombed, convinced in their own minds that the first of the Target Indicators had been laid. The resulting explosions convinced many others already in the target area to bomb, including at least four Squadron aircraft from 101 that completed the outward leg of their journey almost a full half hour before the allotted time.

Meanwhile, Alexander sauntered on.

"Bomb doors open," cried Norman.

"Bomb doors open," Alexander repeated.

Alexander could hear the voice of the Master Bomber, Wing Commander R.J. Lane DSO DFC of 405 Squadron, the Canadians, coming through on the headset, exhorting the

PFF crews to achieve a better concentration for their TIs. His comments were, in Alexander's mind at least, of little real value.

Norman looked through his bomb sight, lining up the cross hairs on a section of three green target indicators he had seen falling moments before. As soon as the PFF flares were released, they were whipped away in the fierce winds such that their final resting place ended far from the actual intended aiming point. Alexander was a stickler for routine and discipline; he had been ordered to bomb at 22.30, and at precisely 22.30 and at a height of 22,000ft Norman pressed the bomb release.

"Bombs gone!"

The aircraft lurched upwards as the weight of its heavy explosive and incendiaries fell from its belly. Then the 30 second wait for the photo. Taffy confirmed the photoflash had successfully flared.

"Bomb doors closed."

"Bomb doors closed," Alexander chanted.

Now let's get out of here Norman thought. Pull your finger out. And yet still Alexander flew on, his indicated airspeed only a fraction above 145 mph, and seemingly in no rush to leave the target area. Curly was almost beside himself. All through the journey, just as Curly adjusted the throttle settings for maximum fuel economy and to have the four Merlins beautifully in tune, Alexander would start meddling. The Lancaster would start vibrating, the noise inside the aircraft would increase noticeably, and Curly's calculations would go to pot. He really had had enough, but as a lowly Sergeant didn't feel particularly well placed to criticise a Wing Commander seven ranks his senior! Alec was also concerned. Standard procedure after the target picture was taken was down with the nose and get the hell out of there. He would allow for the increased speed in calculating when he had to turn onto the next course. Now his calculations had similarly been adversely affected.

While Alexander flew on seemingly without a care in the world, other men in his Squadron were having a torrid time. Sergeant Harnish, a Canadian in a predominantly Canadian crew, lost his starboard outer and was forced to jettison part of his payload shortly after crossing the Danish coast in order to maintain height. He bombed at 22.34, but from a height of only 17,500ft – a full 5,000ft lower than most of his colleagues and placing him uncomfortably close to the flak. He did better than Flying Officer McKenna, however, who overshot the target, seeing the first Pathfinder flares go down at 22.36 – but 20 miles astern of his aircraft! After attempting to battle his way back to the target, he was unable to locate the aiming point at all and in the end, bombed what he believed to be Halberstadt at 23.07.

At last Alexander headed for home, on a course given to him by Alec. They were now heading into the strong winds that had pushed them to the target too early. Despite grievous losses to several nightfighters, and many aircraft succumbing to flak, for Ted and the others it was a quiet, uneventful trip home. Alec had completed another excellent job of navigation, all the more remarkable given the exceptional conditions they faced, and the absence of H2S to help him. When they eventually called Flying Control and entered the circuit to land, most of the crews had already returned, hardly surprising given the early bombing times.

The interrogation proved a livelier affair than usual. At this stage, no-one had ever experienced the phenomenon known as the 'jet stream' which had been responsible for forcing so many of the bombers South off track, and which on the return leg had proved fatal to so many. Some aircraft, it would be learned later, had even strayed over the Ruhr. Although a success was claimed by Bomber Command that night, it was somewhat muted. Most of the returning crews reported heavy flak and fighters, and few were confident they had hit the target. Many complained of poor and scattered marking and the 'lateness' of the Pathfinders. (In fact the Pathfinders had not been late, but had stuck rigidly to the plan. The marking was scattered because of the high winds, which resulted in the greatest concentration of bombs falling at least six miles from the aiming point – the centre of the City).

Although the crew of A *Wing and a Prayer* saw little or nothing worthy of report, the cost to Bomber Command had been high. Some 72 aircraft had been lost, only six fewer than the disaster at Leipzig a few weeks before, and probably as many as 50 of these losses were accountable to flak. Remarkably, every one of the 25 crews from 101 Squadron that set out that night returned safely.

The raid on Berlin on 24th March took Ted's tally of operations to 15, and was the last main force attack mounted on that City by Bomber Command. The Battle of Berlin Play was now all-but over, but it still had one dreadful Act to come.

Meanwhile the Squadron put up four crews for a raid on the railway yards at Aulnoye, an unspectacular operation that missed the target but fortunately didn't result in any losses to the 197 aircraft that took part. It is only worthy of mention, because included in the quartet from 101 despatched that evening was Air Commodore Cozens, the Station Commander at nearby Hemswell (for a period the home of one of the new self-explanatory Lancaster Finishing Schools). Iliffe Cozens was a regular officer and a keen amateur cameraman. He had only a few weeks previously completed a film which was to be used in training to prepare new aircrew in what to expect on a 'typical' bombing sortie. The footage followed Flight Lieutenant Bob Chandler and his crew before, during and after a raid on Berlin, and was especially remarkable because it was shot entirely in colour, from some film that he had somehow managed to scrounge. (The film, entitled *Night Bombers*, is now widely known, and first shown by the BBC in the late 1970s).

Another day and another Battle Order, but Curly was feeling decidedly under the weather. He had been up half the night with an upset tummy and had a real concern for letting the others down in the air if he was caught short. It was also medically unwise. At height, the discomfort of an upset stomach was multiplied considerably and Curly could find himself quite literally doubled up in pain. Against his better judgement, he allowed the others to persuade him to go. After all, he didn't want them to think he'd gone LMF did he?

The target was an old favourite – Essen, in the heart of the ironically-named 'Happy Valley'. The good news about Essen was that it was a much shorter trip than, for example, to Berlin. The bad news was that its defences were legendary in their ferocity, protecting the industrial might of The Fatherland, the steelworks that built the ships and tanks and guns needed to sustain a war and Hitler's ambitions.

Although briefed for clear weather, there was 10/10ths cloud almost all the way, and the force of just over 700 aircraft left a string of contrails in the sky. Harry spotted an Me 110 twin-engined nightfighter over the target as it flashed by at more than 300 mph. Luckily it didn't see them. He informed Rusty. Rusty awaited his instructions. The gunners held their fire, not wanting to give their position away unnecessarily. The 110 was originally designed as a day-fighter. Heavily-armed, and with a crew of three, after some initial successes the *Zerstörer* (destroyer) aircraft failed to live up to its reputation, and was relegated to the ranks of the Nacht Jäger where it came into its own. With two 30mm and two 20 mm canon, it packed an almighty punch, and with some aircraft fitted with upward firing canon (*Schräge Musik* – literally 'slanting music' or Jazz) its successes steadily mounted. Many of the great Nightfighter 'aces' (*Experten*) – Lent, Schnaufer etc – plied their trade with the Me 110, between them building a fearful tally of downed men and machines.

Norman was once again in his element, with lots of fireworks to keep him happy. Again he was giving a running commentary to Rusty, describing the wonderfully large blue-green explosions he could see in the target area below, mixed with the red and green target indicators that had been dropped by Pathfinder Mosquitoes shortly before H-Hour at 22.00.

Ted continued scanning the nightfighter frequencies, but there was little activity on his screen. Despite all the excitement and the intensity of the flak, there was a noticeable absence of nightfighter activity. The German controllers had been caught completely off-guard, and were failing to make any interceptions of note.

By now, however, Curly was in real trouble. The moment they had taken off he had regretted the decision. His worst fears had come true. As they had climbed to operational height, the air outside had become thinner and reduced in pressure. The pressure in his body, however, had remained at ground level. The difference in this air pressure meant that the wind had to escape somehow. Everyone endured the same. Rusty claimed he could tell at what height they were flying by who had farted. Unfortunately, when it came to Curly's turn, it was more than just wind he passed.

He tried to make it down to the Elsan toilet but was too late. He eventually made it, moving down the interior of the aircraft carrying his portable oxygen bottle, all the time watching the gauge lest it should fall below a 'critical' level. It was a good job that he was, because his bottle had a leak, and he was forced to keep stopping to 'top up' at various crew positions. Curly cleaned himself up as best he could but the others were not impressed, and the air that was circulating inside was far from pleasant. He soldiered on.

Landing back at base at 00.45, his 'friends' gave him a wide berth and sat as far away from him as they could in the crew bus. He was treated like a leper, and worse was to come at interrogation. By the time Curly arrived, word had already got out.

"He was so frightened he shat himself!"

They all laughed. Indeed for some days after, Curly endured the sniggers of his crew mates and others on the squadron. He was even convinced at the next Station dance that all the WAAFs were pointing at him, knowingly.

Ted and the others were happy to learn that again there were no casualties on the Squadron – the third trip in a row that the Squadron had come through unscathed. But the balance sheet was about to be horrifically redressed, in a battle that Rusty would later describe in his diary as 'Wholesale Slaughter.'

Thursday 30th March was like any other day for Bomber Command. The Commander-in-Chief, Harris, convened his usual 9-00am conference and three quarters of an hour later the meeting had concluded with a decision to bomb Nuremberg.

Why Nuremberg was chosen has been discussed in detail in many other titles, notably Martin Middlebrook's 'The Nuremberg Raid', and James Campbell's more controversial volume, 'The Bombing of Nuremberg'. In simple terms, there appears to be two factors influencing the decision: the weather, and what can only be described as Harris' 'obstinacy'.

For a raid to be successful, certain weather conditions were obviously required and desired. Firstly the weather had to be suitably benign to allow 800-plus aircraft to take-off from a variety of air-bases all over the country, and climb to height without the danger of icing. Once over the target area, the weather would ideally be clear (especially if beyond the range of Oboe – the blind-bombing system) for the Pathfinders to mark the target and enable the Main Force to bomb. Most importantly, there had to be no fog, and a reasonably high cloud base for landing. There was little point in sending out a Force if they then couldn't be recovered, as Bomber Command found to its cost on 'Black Thursday' as mentioned earlier.

The conditions reported at the conference were complicated, and immediately out-of-date as soon as they arrived. To the best of the Met Officers knowledge, however, the conditions being reported to him and being updated by weather flights meant options were severely restricted. A raid on any target town in the North of Germany was out of the question because of cloud coming down from the North Sea and large clear areas in-land which would expose the Bombers to fighter attack. The moon was also a factor. Ordinarily it would have been too late in the moon period to consider operations at all but the possibility of high cloud behind the cold front which might conceal the Bomber stream led Harris to consider the South.

Then came Harris obstinacy. Schweinfurt and Regensburg, two targets on his priority list as part of the Pointblank directive could, and arguably should, have been first choice targets. For whatever reason which will never truly be known and only subject to supposition, Harris looked elsewhere. He wanted instead an Area target, a major industrial City that his Bombers could hit and get results after the relative disappointments and losses in the most recent attacks. There was one obvious choice, shining out at him like a beacon, and ironically placed half-way between Schweinfurt and Regensburg. The City was Nuremberg. It was the obvious choice. And why should he attack it? Because it was there.

Soon the Bomber Command machine swung into operation. The Telexes began chattering, and a call from No 1 Group to Ludford Magna shortly after 10-00am that morning required a 'Goodwood' (maximum effort) on 'Grayling', the code-name for Nuremberg. Across Ludford, the Station came alive. They had not operated for three days now, and the evening before a trip to Brunswick had been scrubbed at the last minute. There was a need to keep the momentum going.

The Intelligence Officer was especially busy. Nuremberg had not been raided since the Autumn of 1943, and target material was not easy to come by. Nuremberg, he discovered, was 'The most German of German Cities,' according to the Austrian Adolf Hitler. Hitler chose Nuremberg as the venue for the annual convention for his National Socialist Party – the infamous show-piece 'rallies' broadcast on the news-reels of healthy young Aryan Germans proclaiming their lives to their Fatherland and their Führer. In 1935, Nuremberg was also the venue for the equally infamous 'Nürnberg Laws' which divided the people of Germany into three classes: German (Aryan) citizens enjoying full rights; Jews who had two or more Jewish grandparents and who were excluded from the ordinary rights of citizenship, could not marry Germans, and who were virtually condemned to a Ghetto existence; and 'mixed' or 'hybrid' persons who had one or two Jewish grandparents, were not of Jewish faith or married to a

Jew, and who might marry Germans and become assimilated into the German people.

The historic City, home to fabulous 11th Century Kaiser-schloss and Italian-style Rathaus containing frescos by Albert Dürer, was also home to some 425.529 (1939 figure) Germans. Of more interest from the IO's perspective, however, were the industries that the City supported, including the MAN heavy-engineering works, two Siemens electrical factories and a small aircraft repair facility on the outskirts of Fürth.

Ted and the others had had a good night's sleep, their third in succession. Only Harry was suffering. They had been briefed the previous evening to go to Brunswick, as stated, and Harry had decided to take two of the 'Wakey Wakey' pills to keep him alert. Firstly there was a postponement, and a delay, while Bomber Command made its final decision. The delay was such that shortly before they were due to take-off, Harry slipped another couple of pills inside him with a glass of water and waited for the 'go'. At the eleventh hour, the operation was scrubbed, leaving Harry pacing the billet all night, muttering to himself, totally unable to sleep!

It was a bright but chilly morning as Rusty wandered over to the Flight Office to see whether anything was happening, fully expecting to be stood down, or at least allocated some practice flying. There was concern when they were told that operations were indeed 'on' for that night, and the preliminary briefing had been set for 15.00. None of them had any real sense of foreboding, but the decision certainly raised an eyebrow or two amongst the older 'sweats'.

Their humour was not helped by the activities going on around them. The planned raid on Brunswick the evening before and its subsequent cancellation meant many of the bombers had been left with their bomb-loads intact – only the fuses had been removed. The combination of bomb and fuel loads indicated a long trip; now some of the bombs were being winched down from the bomb bays to make room for the weight of additional fuel. Wherever they were headed, it was going to be deep into enemy territory, with a bright moon to help the fighters.

Some of the aircrew killed time by wandering off to the local farmhouse for a fry-up whilst Curly and Ted rode over to dispersal to see Jock and the lads. Harry sat cross-legged on his bed in his long-johns, practising his clarinet. (He had earlier lost his reed, only to discover it later, sliced in two, damaged beyond repair. He had rightfully accused Taffy who as usual denied all knowledge that he had been anywhere near the scene of the crime.)

The Squadron and Flight Commanders meanwhile worked out who would go. The Battle Order No 491 that appeared detailed 26 crews for operations. It would be the biggest effort from a single squadron that night.

Rusty read down the list: P/O Adamson, S/L Morton, F/S Arnold, P/O Corkill, F/L Todd, P/O Waughman, F/L Goeres, F/O McKenna, F/S Davidson, P/O Lander, F/S Harnish, F/S McHattie, W/O Drew, F/S Fillingham, F/S Thomas, F/S King, F/O Wallis, F/O Hall, P/O Batten-Smith, P/O Rowe, F/O Davies, F/S Tivey, P/O Holland, F/S Bateman, F/L Knights, P/O Irving. The Squadron was making a maximum effort, he noted, more than 200 men. What he didn't know was that many would pay the ultimate price.

The hours and the minutes passed agonisingly slowly by, until at last, late into the afternoon they assembled for briefing, and after the usual, slightly forced banter and the entrance of the senior commanders, the Intelligence Officer mounted the rostrum to reveal the target for tonight: Nuremberg.

114

Some groaned; some catcalled. Others remained impassive, deep in thought. Nuremberg. Three times further into enemy territory than any target in the Ruhr. A total journey of more than 1,000 miles, much of it across a hostile landmass, without the comfort of the North Sea for a 'safer' entry or exit. By now Rusty's eyes – and 200 other sets of eyes – had been drawn to the unusually long ribbon in the centre of the map, passing close – uncomfortably close – to the Ruhr and the Frankfurt defences. He also noted the nightfighter stations, and the beacons around which the fighters gathered to receive their orders to attack. Alec's navigation would have to be spot on if they were not to drift off target and into the welcoming arms of the very worst the Luftwaffe and Flak could throw at them. Alec had completed his calculations earlier. His figures made unpleasant reading; a 'Long Leg' of more than 250 miles through one of the best defended areas of Germany. Still, he thought, they would at least have the comfort of cloud cover most of the way to the target. After all, the Met Officer had assured them of such hadn't he? And although there would be cloud to protect them on the way in, the target area should be largely clear which meant that Norman would have a clear view of the aiming point.

After the specialists had had their say, and following a customary 'Good Luck' from the CO, Rusty and the others began gathering their flight bags and the usual paraphernalia in preparation for the 'off'. There wasn't much talking as they began to clamber into their flying kit. They, nor any of the other crews operating that night, could have had any sense of impending catastrophe. Nor did they know of the irony that one of the men who had been with Harris that morning in deciding the target for that night had been none other than their former Squadron Commander, Group Captain George Carey-Foster.

The bus dropped them at their aircraft. Rusty exchanged the usual conversation with Jock. He didn't ask where they were going. He never did. But the crew always made a point of telling them where they'd been. The lads would call to Alec to cover his maps and charts if they had to come on board to resolve any last minute issues. Rusty had already signed the Form 700 that said his aircraft was 'fit for purpose', having air-tested the Lancaster earlier in the day. Now they waited for the start-up time which finally arrived. The port inner crack-led into life, followed by the other three engines until all four Merlins were running smoothly. With the signal to move off, the groundcrew pulled the restraining chocks away and Rusty released the brakes, rolling the mighty aircraft forward onto the perimeter track at the head of a long snaking queue of aircraft meandering towards the take-off point.

Rusty wheeled the aircraft to line her up facing the runway (unusually running north to south) and await the 'green' of the Aldis lamp from the chequered controller's caravan to his left. Then it came, and Rusty called for full power as man, machine and munitions thundered along the runway, at first threatening never to leave the ground and then, with the airfield boundary fast approaching, finally becoming unstuck and taking almost unwillingly it seemed into the air. The nose of the aircraft dipped slightly as the undercarriage came up and the two green lights on the panel winked out as the gear locked. It was 21.35.

As A Wing and a Prayers' speed and height increased, climbing on full power to 2,000ft before finally throttling back, behind them the next of the 101 Squadron aircraft flown by Flying Officer McKenna was also completing its take-off run and lifting skywards. He in turn was followed by Squadron Leader Morton and Pilot Officer Corkill, in an act that would be repeated 26 times until the final Squadron aircraft (Pilot Officer 'Dutch' Holland in H – How) was airborne. The aircraft that had been orbiting in the clear skies at a safe height and distance, and with their navigation lights switched on (the threat of collision was considered greater than the threat from German Intruders) now began to head towards the assembly point. Each had an allotted time at this point over the North Sea, for the ABC aircraft were to be integrated throughout the Main Stream, five to a wave, to ensure a consistency of jamming.

A *Wing and a Prayer* continued to climb steadily though the clear skies. Harry, for one of only a few occasions he could remember, could actually see several other Lancasters behind him in a loose formation. It was nice to have friendly company for a change. He hoped visibility wouldn't be so favourable over Germany.

The aircraft crossed the Suffolk coast shortly after 23.15 and Harry and Tommy asked permission to test their weapons. Norman did the same. He was as usual already in the bomb aimer's position to help Alec with a pin point, and for once could quite easily make out the welcoming English coastline that they would shortly be leaving behind and crossing another coast, a deadlier coast, and just how deadly they were about to find out.

Curly had synchronised the engines to be running in perfect pitch, keeping a watchful eye on the flickering dials, and Rusty engaged the automatic pilot, George. It would be a long flight, and it was sensible to use those tools that were there to assist whenever possible. Taffy was bored. There was little for him to do except wait for the wind broadcasts from Group. Behind him, Ted switched on the ABC equipment, making sure it was nicely warmed up and working properly before crossing the Belgium shores.

"Enemy Coast Ahead."

It was Norman. Less than 15 minutes after reaching the Assembly Point they were now over the enemy coast, and only a further 20 minutes flying time from their first turning point, the little mining town of Charleroi. Another 18 minutes on from there, and according to Alec's calculations they would be over the German frontier.

"Turning point coming up skipper," Alec called. "Steer new course …"

'W' flew on due east from Charleroi. Now the long leg. More than 220 miles. At least one hour's flying time. The first flak appeared, but well off target, and only very light. It would be much warmer later.

Blips began to appear on Ted's cathode ray tubes, a more ominous sign of enemy activity. "The fighters are on their way," he said, and as he did so began moving the dials and pressing the key that would hopefully drown out the German instructions.

Norman fidgeted. Although he appeared to enjoy operations and the spectacular panorama during a raid, the sound of Ted's voice calling from the depths of the aircraft to announce fighters always scared him. He must say so at some time; stop him doing it, he thought.

So far, the trip had been uneventful, but Rusty was concerned about the conditions. The moon was well up, and they could see for literally miles around. It was virtually daylight – ideal nightfighter weather. They wouldn't need Radar, they would be able to see their targets for themselves.

Disaster had already befallen a 101 Squadron aircraft, and in tragic circumstances. The Lancaster of Pilot Officer Bill Adamson DFC and his experienced crew, on their 29th and penultimate operation, was mistaken for an enemy aircraft by the rear gunner of a 'friendly' Halifax who opened fire with a long burst of tracer. The Lancaster (DV264 'L') was fatally hit.

Four managed to successfully bail out, the bomb aimer, wireless op, mid-upper gunner and Special Duties Operator. The latter, the 24-year old Mancunian Flying Officer Norman Marrian, who had been wounded in the attack, was found two days later, still hanging in his parachute harness, dead.

It was the first, but unfortunately only the start of a terrible night for 101, and their second aircraft to fall followed shortly after. Flight Sergeant Len Lockwood, the navigator on Lancaster LL832 K$_2$ flown by Flight Sergeant Gerald Tivey, a 22-year old Derby man on his 10th Operation, found himself horribly off-course. He was by no means alone. Weather conditions and wind-speeds had not been as forecast, and he was now many miles South of their planned route. Whereas for others that night, such a deviation from the Main Force whether intentionally or not would prove their salvation, Lockwood had the misfortune of guiding his aircraft over the heavily defended town of Coblenz. They were hit by flak and crashed by the village of Rübenach at 00.15. There were no survivors.

101 had therefore lost two of its vital ABC aircraft before it had even reached the Rhine. But they were by no means the only ones suffering. Tivey's crew was the 17th bomber to be shot down, and the Germans had only just started.

Suddenly there was an explosion in the night sky, to the starboard, south of the Ruhr. And then shortly after, another. Bluish tracer trails could be seen clearly, arcing towards a target and then disappearing, consumed by the explosion they had created.

"Lancaster in trouble on port beam."

"There another one on fire. Jesus look at that."

Voices were on the intercom. Expressions of horror and disbelief as another and then another aircraft was plucked from the stream. Alec noted the positions of fallen aircraft as accurately as he could. Rusty has counted 16; Alec several more. They stopped counting. 'W' flew on.

By now it was clear that the enemy was having a successful night. As fast as Ted found a frequency and jammed it, another appeared on his scope. The 101 Squadron Special Duties Operators were being worked to the limit. 26 men jamming three frequencies each: 78 interceptions. And yet still the German Fighter Controllers' instructions were coming through loud and clear. The ABC aircraft were too few in number, and spread too thinly throughout the stream to have any serious impact. They were now down to 24. And they were rapidly losing more of their number.

Fifty miles to the North, another 101 Squadron aircraft was in trouble. Flying Officer Mervyn Hutchinson, a 28-year old New Zealander and the navigator on K-King was lost. His error proved fatal. They probably never saw the nightfighter that accounted for them. Certainly the action was brief and decisive, with the bomber crashing from 18,000ft near Dillenberg, 20 miles South East of Siegen. Miraculously, two of the crew were thrown clear and survived – the Pilot, Pilot Officer Albert Lander, and the wireless operator, Sergeant Clapp.

More aircraft went down. But it was not all one-sided. Rusty spotted at least one bomber get the better of an enemy fighter. The Germans weren't having it all their own way.

Alec reported: "Two minutes to turning point."

They were now fast approaching the last leg of the journey, a short right hand turn and then 75 miles to the target. Alec's navigation was again spot on. They made the turn slightly north of the Thüringer Wald, 10 minutes behind the front of the stream at approximately 00.55.

Nearly 60 aircraft had now been shot down from the Main Force, mostly the experienced crews flying in the second and third waves of the attack. Those at the front of the attack had got through virtually unscathed. Those behind would be similarly unmolested. But if the bombers thought the last turn would throw the Germans off the scent, they were to be bitterly disappointed, and for one crew fatally so.

Donald Irving was on his 9th operation. It was his last. He was at least 50 miles off course and 10 miles north of Eisenach when the nightfighter, an Me 110 piloted by Hauptmann Gustav Tham of IV./NJG V struck. Irving, a 26-year old Australian from New South Wales stood no chance. The bomber crashed with such terrific force with its full bomb load including a 4,000lb cookie intact that no trace of the crew could be found. Five other Australians, an English Flight Engineer and a Canadian SDO died with him.

Still 'W' flew on. And still Ted attempted to prevent a rout from becoming a slaughter. But the Germans were learning. In the first half of the attack, the German's Third Fighter Division's controller had assembled his aircraft around a fighter beacon – 'Ida' – South East of Cologne. The stream also had to pass a second radio beacon – Otto – before the last turn. Every available fighter was being thrown into the assault by means of the running commentary. The Germans were switching between nine different speech channels and two Morse channels; at the height of the battle, the running commentary was being broadcast on five separate channels. Ted found them, but the transmissions were so powerful, and so many frequencies being utilised, that his jamming was having little effect. There was also the point that they had now lost three ABC aircraft, and were about to lose their fourth.

Flight Sergeant Robertson, navigator to Flight Sergeant Clyde Harnish on only his 6th operation was bang on course. Like many others in the stream, however, he was a victim of the bizarre weather conditions that resulted in condensation trails streaming from his aircraft. The white vapour, clearly visible in the moonlit sky, drew the German nightfighters to their prey with commensurate ease. It was a bonanza time, especially for Leutnant Wilhelm Suess.

Suess was one of the first exponents of *Schräge Musik*, the upward firing cannon, and he was looking for his third 'kill' of the night. But Harnish wasn't going to oblige so easily. As the German opened fire, Harnish began corkscrewing feverishly, desperately trying to lose the fighter. Unfortunately Suess was an old hand, and managed to re-formate under the weaving bomber unseen and fire again. Now he set the bomber's wings on fire, igniting the incendiaries in the bomb bay. Harnish did all he could to extinguish the flames, including the last desperate gamble of plunging the bomber into a steep dive, but all to no avail. Harnish just managed to retain sufficient control of the burning bomber to allow five of the crew to escape, before it spun into the ground and exploded in the village of Simmerhausen, 12 miles East of Fulda.

They had not yet reached the target and already 101 Squadron had lost five of its number. And the night was far from finished.

At 00.58 precisely, the raid on Nuremberg began. Over the next 25 minutes, the attack went spectacularly wrong. Despite the best efforts of the Pathfinders, heavy cloud over the target and much stronger than forecast winds pushed many of the bombers off course and put paid to accurate marking. Certainly some of the markers fell on Nuremberg, but a good many fell further to the East, and the small town of Lauf.

With the attack officially due to open at 01.10 at a rate of 160 tons of bombs a minute, only three aircraft were on time. Over the next five minutes, only a further 33 aircraft completed their runs. Within this number was the Canadian Flying Officer Goeres, whose bomb aimer Flight Sergeant

Roy bombed at three minutes after H-Hour at 21,000ft on the pre-determined heading of 175 Magnetic. He could see little Pathfinder activity, and only a handful of burning incendiaries. Moments later, Flying Officer Neale, bomb aimer with Flying Officer McKenna, also called 'bombs gone', noting both the TI markers and the Release Point flares apparently in a line running East to West across the target. It was to be a familiar story at the later debriefing, Flight Sergeant McHattie reporting much the same phenomena. McKenna's aircraft was carrying one of the 4,000 bombs with a 35-hour time delay to cause maximum disruption, hopefully just when the German rescue workers thought it was safe.

As they attacked, the SDOs, Flying Officer Cooper and Sergeant Smith respectively, could clearly hear the German fighter controller exhorting his crews to steer 'Nach Nürnberg'. Ted picked up a similar transmission – and hit the jamming key.

Flying Officer Connell, bomb aimer with Flight Sergeant Fillingham and crew was next to bomb at 01.16.

As Connell held his aircraft steady to complete the bombing run and return the all-important aiming point photograph, Norman was guiding Rusty through his bomb sight onto the target. Norman was one of the lucky ones. Whereas others found the target obscured by cloud, Norman was able to clearly see a concentration of green TIs on the ground and called: "Bombs Gone", marking the time at 01.17. The aircraft surged again as the mighty weight of a 4000lb High Capacity bomb fell from the bomb bay and Norman checked his control panel to ensure that all the munitions had been successfully discharged. As he did so, both he and Rusty saw a terrific explosion, some way East of the target. They didn't know it then, but what they were witnessing was almost certainly the lucky hit on an ammunition train in-between Nuremberg and Lauf.

Also witness to the explosion was the 'C' Flight Commander, Squadron Leader Morton, whose bomb aimer, Flight Lieutenant Bradley, similarly logged his bombing time at 01.17.

The seconds ticked by. Still only a trickle of the Main Force had bombed. Many were still off track; only a handful were getting through.

Flying Officer Hall as part of his payload had a cookie with a three-day time delay. He wanted to ensure it found a suitable target, and was satisfied when his bomb aimer, Flight Sergeant Taggart, bombed the centre of a cluster of eight RP flares red with yellow stars cascading from 22,000ft. There was already a good concentration of fires that he would add to.

A *Wing and a Prayer* turned for home, Rusty opening up the taps, the crew still very much on the qui vive, anxious to leave the carnage behind. The moon had lost most of its intensity now, and it was getting darker, but the night still held fear. Harry, in particular, was concerned. He hadn't told his skipper, but his electrically-heated suit had packed up long-since, and he was exposed quite literally to the elements. Stuck out in the tail, he stood a very real chance of freezing to death. But he didn't complain. It wasn't the form, and anyway everybody else was busy.

The last bomb to fall on Nuremberg was recorded at 01.21, at the precise time that Warrant Officer Drewy completed his run over the city, only to learn later that the target he attacked was almost certainly Lauf, albeit well marked with flares.

Any crews later than this, almost certainly missed, a fact reinforced by the confused and contradictory reports at interrogation.

Pilot Officer Corkill came in over the target at 150 IAS, and his bomb aimer Flight Sergeant Gundy aimed at a concentrated group of Pathfinder flares in large numbers. He could not, however see the ground – only the glows of the fires through the cloud. It was 01.22. Also seeing fire glows on the cloud was the Canadian bomb aimer in V_2, Flight Sergeant Cuthbert, piloted by Flying Officer Wallis, a contemporary of Rusty's in 'C' Flight. In his opinion, however, marking was scattered. Flight Sergeant King, also bombing at 01.22 reported a concentration of fires west of his target.

Another 'C' Flight aircrew, skippered by Flying Officer Oliver Davies, attacked from 21,000ft, bombing the centre of four red TIs seen on the ground, but also seeing bomb bursts scattered North West of the target. Some, including Flight Sergeant Bateman and Flight Lieutenant Knights, despite a good aiming point and certain of their targets, bombed and missed without knowing it. Others realised their error at the time.

One of these was Flight Lieutenant Todd, who had as his navigator arguably one of the most experienced men on the raid, Squadron Leader Rosevear. They, like many others, were now considerably off course but unaware. Assuming their navigation to be spot on, they had every reason to believe that Schweinfurt was Nuremberg – it was the same distance and flying time from the turning point that they had predicted. Unfortunately, they had made their last turn far to the North of where they should have been, hence the confusion. They also didn't have the benefit of H2S. This confusion was further compounded by the fact that although they couldn't see any Pathfinder flares – they assumed they were late – they did see the flashes of bombs from many other aircraft exploding below. In the absence of markers, the bomb aimer, Sergeant

Bardell, chose as his target the flak and searchlight positions, letting them have the full payload of heavy explosive and incendiaries. As they turned for home, he then had the horror of seeing a number of red TIs 20-30 miles on the port beam, and the full realisation of what they had done began to dawn.

In one of the most remarkable incidents for the Squadron that night, Sergeant Alderson, the bomb aimer in a novice crew skippered by Flight Sergeant Davidson, was most unhappy with his aiming point. Believing the RP flares to be fakes, perhaps part of some German ruse, he aborted the first run and went 'round again! Still not entirely satisfied, he bombed the centre of a scattered group of Pathfinder flares, but on checking his indicator panel for hang ups was horrified to see that the largest munition, a 2,000lb bomb, had not released and despite every effort from his pilot the bomb refused to budge.

While Davidson was struggling, another 101 Squadron pilot was about to die. Unknown to the ever-popular and experienced Pilot Officer John Batten-Smith DFC on his 22nd Operation, Helmut Schulte, an Oberleutnant with II/NJG5, was about to end his life, and that of his crew whose average age was only 21. A long burst of canon and machine-gun fire despatched the Lancaster in seconds, spinning out of control and crashing by the side of the Autobahn almost equidistant from Nuremberg and Lauf.

By now, A Wing and a Prayer, lightened of her load, had increased speed significantly. It had taken less than four hours' flying to reach the target, but now they were flying into wind, and faced a long, tortuous journey home. The only blessing was that the intensity of the German attacks had decreased. The broadcasts from the German Controllers had not finished, but Ted noticed they had become less frequent. None of them had any real idea how big a tragedy had befallen Bomber Command that night, and even less idea how significant the loss was going to be to their own Squadron. And still, there was one more desperate act to come.

Shortly after 05.15, 'W' made her landfall at Selsey Bill. Rusty had called up on VHF and identified his aircraft while they were still short of the English Coast. They had taken to singing 'Coming home on a Wing and a Prayer' as they neared home as a form of release, but nobody felt much like it now.

Another hour and they should be home; they could look out for the friendly Pundit beacon that flashed in morse code the identification letter of Ludford Magna. Ahead of them, Flight Sergeant Edwin Thomas was in trouble. Thomas was another 'C' Flight pilot, a 26-year old married man from Forest Gate. Whether he was wounded, or his aircraft badly damaged is not known. What is known is that in attempting to land at a US Transport & Troop Carrying base near Newbury, Berkshire, he flew his Lancaster into the ground at 05.03. It was the Squadron's seventh loss that night – and Bomber Command's 101st.

Rusty was very tired. Harry was very cold. Both would soon find salvation on the ground. Rusty called the control tower asking for permission to join the circuit and land. He joined four others, and awaited patiently their turn to 'pancake'. Rusty brought the aircraft down to land, and once safely back on mother earth, eased the throttles back as the white-hot exhaust stubs crackled reassuringly. Marshalled into their dispersal, the engines were shut down, and the exhausted crew began to clamber out.

Harry was slow to move. He was, almost quite literally, frozen solid. Hanging from his face mask was an icicle, as thick as a wrist, extending from the bottom of his chin to his lap where the spittle had drained out and frozen. His face was also severely frost bitten, but still he didn't complain, although it would later mean a long spell in 'dock'.

Conversation was difficult. None of them had ever experienced anything like that before. They felt shaken. Alec had taken to keeping a book on the number of aircraft shot down. All of them chipped five shillings a piece into a pool, winner takes all. He asked Curly for his guess.

"I saw up to 60 and then lost count," Curly said. "I reckon we lost at least a hundred."

The crew bus came to take them to debriefing. The Station Intelligence Officers began working through the laborious report sheets, but the conversation was all about the losses. The Intelligence staff were dismissive of the wild guesses being thrown around of how many aircraft had been short down. The tension rose, and there were unpleasant, angry scenes which again none of them had witnessed before.

The briefing over, the crews returned to their respective messes, still unaware of the extent of the Squadron losses but with a sense of foreboding. Norman in particular was looking forward to his eggs and bacon – it was always welcome. Walking into the dining room, however, he was surprised to find the room devoid of any of the WAAF girls who were usually there with a friendly smile and a greeting to serve them their meal. The serving cabinet was filled with eggs, already fried, as well as the customary bacon and fried bread but there were no waitresses. Instead there was a notice pinned to the wall that simply instructed them to help themselves. The WAAFs already knew the full cost to the Squadron in human lives, but were unable to accept the reality of so many of 'their' boys not coming back. They were in the rest room, in tears.

Norman wanted to go in and say something, try and comfort them, but the WAAF NCO told him it was better that they were left alone. At last a handful did come out, with pain and grief etched on their tear-stained faces. It was something none of them would ever forget. Wearily, they retired to bed. Rusty picked up his diary and penned a few lines in the boxed area marked Thursday 30th March.

"Heaviest losses yet. We lost seven. Quite a blow. All of us were pretty tired and shaken."

It ended: "Nevertheless we must press on regardless."

Not surprisingly after the disaster of Nuremberg, the Squadron was rested. Seven new crews were brought in to replace the 56 men who were missing, and there were many unfamiliar faces in both the officers' and the sergeants' messes. They were the new boys. Soon they would be integrated seamlessly into Squadron life, and the faces of those who had died would be a memory. Gone, but never forgotten, not least by those who now counted themselves lucky to have survived, Alec in particular. He, like Rusty, had recently 'put up a ring'. Unlike Rusty, however, he had had to borrow the money for his new uniform from his father until his official 'allowance' had been paid into his account. He bought his new uniform from Simpsons, and with his promotion came the transfer to the officers' mess. Alec was convinced more than ever that their survival was primarily about luck. He didn't dwell on it, but he nevertheless kept his little doll and lucky silk scarf close to hand – just in case.

On the Saturday, Ted and the others celebrated All Fools Day with a 45 minute air test in 'W'. Indeed the next week was spent in local flying, fighter affiliation and cross country exercises.

At about this time, a step-change was occurring in Bomber Command's strategy. The invasion of Normandy by the Allies would commence in less than 10 weeks. Whereas Harris' doctrine had been to smash the German war effort to his own agenda, he now found a new directive for his Squadrons – to bomb targets in support of the invasion effort. Over the period of the next few weeks and months, targets would change from the major Cities in favour of 'strategic' objectives such as railheads, ammunition dumps, coastal gun batteries and radio and radar installations. At about this time, a directive also came down from the Air Ministry to the Squadrons that because the distances covered to targets in Belgium and Northern France were that much shorter than to those in the heart of Germany, the risk was considered less, and therefore such sorties would only count as one third of an operation is respect of an operational tour. The identity of the individual who initiated this ridiculous and ludicrous move has been blurred somewhat with the passage of time, but in 1944 the Bomber Command crews had no doubts in their minds as to what sort of man he was.

On 9th April the Squadron was back on operations, flying a one-third trip to Lille and Villeneuve-St-Georges, attacking goods stations and railway yards. They flew again to Aulnoye the next day, losing one crew skippered by Flight Lieutenant Nimmo (although he and three others would survive and evade capture). The following week they did the same, to Rouen, but this time *A Wing and a Prayer* was with them.

The attack was a complete success. There was no moon and only moderate to light flak. The need for accuracy brought the bombing height down considerably, and Rusty and Norman working between them bombed at 9,000ft at a speed of more than 220 mph. Their bombs fell short by a mere 100 yards, and the destruction of the yard was virtually complete. More good news was that not a single one of the 273 Lancasters and 16 Mosquitoes taking part in the raid were lost, although there was some excitement while 'W' was in the circuit awaiting its turn to land.

German listening stations monitored R/T traffic during the morning, and had a fair indication if a raid was planned for that night by the volume of traffic received as each wireless operator tested his set. This meant they occasionally sent long-range fighters with drop-tanks to patrol known Bomber Command airfields in the hope of catching bombers unawares, especially while they had their navigation lights switched on to help them avoid collisions during take-off and landing.

As he waited at dispersal for the crew's safe return, Jock Steadman could hear the pitch of the Merlins rise and fall as the pilots adjusted the throttles prior to landing. He also thought he heard a different engine noise, but one that wasn't familiar to him. Just then, a twin-engined two-tailed kite flashed across the airfield at 1,000ft. It was an Me110. Indeed there were two, hovering in the night sky waiting to pounce on an unsuspecting Lancaster whose gunners were no longer so alert or had convinced themselves that they were now safe and could relax. It wasn't the Germans' lucky night; both aircraft were shot down.

Thursday 20th April also called for the bombing of railway installations and marshalling yards, but this time back in Germany and specifically Cologne. It was not a maximum effort by any means. Just over 350 Lancasters in all, but again there was plenty of excitement. Earlier in the day, Curly had been messing about with one of the WAAFs. It was just horse-play, but as punishment for his teasing her she had denied him his pre-op extra egg.

"It'll be your fault if I don't come back," he told her, rather cruelly, but still very much in fun.

Unusually, the crew was not flying in 'W' since it was due an inspection, and instead took 'Z' Zebra. They carried a different payload than most of the others: 11 x 1000lb bombs and four 500 pounders. No incendiaries. There was also a new member of the crew. Harry was suffering the effects of nine hours of extreme cold over Nuremberg, and his place as rear gunner was taken by the Gunnery Leader, Flight Lieutenant Sandy Hill. Rusty was happy. He had an experienced man guarding their tail, and if they couldn't have Harry then the gunnery boss was the next best thing.

It was a late evening take-off, and no fewer than 29 crews were detailed for operations. As Rusty made height and headed for the assembly point, searchlights over Hull and Grimsby coned him, and he had to take evasive action. He'd had more than enough of searchlights for one tour. The Germans were bombing the ports, and the crew had the unnerving sight of a Dornier Do217 passing close by them on its way to its target.

The trip out was fairly quiet. The crew were settled, but never relaxed. Norman was disappointed to find 10/10ths cloud on the approach to the City that would make finding the aiming point difficult. They were also now being buffeted by heavy flak. Indeed it was all very unsatisfactory. For some reason they were very late on target – a full 20 minutes behind some of their Squadron crewmates – and were the last to bomb. Norman aimed for the fires, and had the satisfaction of seeing a number of bomb flashes in the target area that would add to the substantial damage caused to the City that night, leaving nearly 2,000 inhabitants killed or injured and a good many industrial premises destroyed. They turned for home.

Back at Ludford Magna, the WAAF who had denied Curly his rations was beside herself with worry. All of the Squadron aircraft had returned some time since, but 'Z' Zebra was now overdue. The other Squadron pilots and aircrew had already been interrogated, eaten and returned to their billets before Zebra finally returned. Rusty had been unable to contact base. When they did finally walk into the Mess, there was an emotional re-union with the tearful WAAF, and the promise never to say such stupid things again. There was an even greater shock for Rusty. He returned to his hut to find his kit being packed by the Committee of Adjustment – those responsible for taking away the personal belongings of those missing in action. In this case, their actions were somewhat previous.

Some humour was restored however by the presence of the BBC. The distinguished reporter Michael North had chosen that night to visit the station and interview returning crews on the succession of that night's operations. It gave them all a tremendous opportunity for plenty of line shooting!

Brunswick, the venue for Ted's third operation was again the target for his 19th, but events were to conspire against them in an incident that has to this day never been satisfactorily resolved.

Take-off was uneventful. They were back in *A Wing and a Prayer* with Sergeant Law sitting in for Harry in the rear turret. Some of the Squadron was briefed for Brunswick, with the majority detailed for a larger raid on Düsseldorf. Just after an hour into their flight, Alec was troubled. The needle on the DR compass was spinning aimlessly.

"Navigator to Pilot."

"Go ahead Alec."

"Skipper, the DR compass is u/s and so's the master unit."

"What about the P4?"

"That's also u/s."

"What are you saying?"

"We could go on with the Gyro, but it's a long way and it's not very reliable. We've already lost the stream and pretty shortly we'll be out of range of Gee."

Rusty, with his typical cool, detached calmness, was weighing up their options. Certainly Alexander would not be impressed to see an 'early return', but if they flew on it would be without the protection of the stream, with no reliable navigational aids except quite literally the stars to guide them, with every possibility that they would miss the target completely. They could all be killed for nothing. Best live to fight another day when the odds were slightly less stacked against you.

"Pilot to crew, we're turning back. Alec get me an astro fix when you can we're heading for home."

There was no more talking. Each man was alone with his thoughts. At 10,000ft, Norman jettisoned two of the American-type 1000lb bombs over the water and they headed West, reaching the English coast and eventually base, arriving back at Ludford, disconsolate, at 02.10.

Alexander had Rusty in his office straight away. He was not a happy man, and demanded to know why they had not "pressed on." Rusty explained that the DR compass had gone u/s.

"Well couldn't you have used the P4?" he thundered.

"No," Rusty replied. "The P4 was u/s too."

Alexander was incredulous. "The P4 never goes faulty," he said. "How do you explain that?"

Rusty couldn't.

"It's not good enough Waughman," Alexander concluded. "In future you must press on whatever happens. Understand?"

Rusty understood, saluted and shuffled out of the door like a schoolboy from a headmaster's office.

Later that day, Jock and the lads made a remarkable discovery. On 'swinging' the aircraft to check the compass, they discovered a series of magnetic links in the chain to the control column. The P4 compass was situated close by the column, and as the aircraft swung, the compass went haywire. They had found the cause, but not the reason, and reported their findings to the Wing Commander. Rusty was summoned to the office again. The Wingco didn't apologise, but patiently explained to Rusty that the cause of his compass failure had been discovered, and that he had in fact been correct in the action he and his crew had taken.

How the links got into the column could not be explained. Some wild theories were thrown about, and it was the subject of much debate in the mess, with talk even of fifth columnists and sabotage. But no-one really knew or ever found out. It remained – and still remains – a mystery.

The disappointment of Brunswick was quickly forgotten about the next day, Sunday 23rd April – St George's Day – celebrated with a football match on a field behind one of the village pubs. All ranks took parts and no-one was especially keeping score, although Flying Officer McKenna particularly impressed with his footballing skills. Or so he thought. The football was followed by a film and an inevitable booze up in their respective messes.

For Ted's 19th trip they were briefed for Munich, heartland of Bavaria. It was by no means a Main Force attack; the majority of bombers that night were to attack Karlsruhr, but it was to be a mammoth of endurance. The routes in and out chosen were via Italy, Switzerland and France, crossing the Alps twice. Norman would enjoy the scenery. If he was lucky he'd see Mont Blanc. Just as long as Rusty didn't fly that close!

In the crew room waiting for the bus to take them to dispersal, Taffy sidled up to Rusty whose back was turned to him.

"I've been drinking," he said, slurring his words deliberately in a mock drunken act, "and I'm going to fly!"

"You fucker!" Rusty retorted, turning around as he did so to be faced by two blushing WAAFs. It provided a brief moment of relief from the tension around.

Take off was at 20.45, and the crew settled down for the long flight ahead. They carried enough fuel for a nine and a half hour flight – and they would need every drop of it. Ted was busy. Attempts to catch the German Controllers unawares had not entirely succeeded and Rusty saw two of the nine Lancasters lost that night plucked from the night sky ahead of him. He also noted another, smaller explosion. The Germans weren't having it all their own way. The gunners were alert. Harry was still sick, so Sergeant Cox had taken the mid-upper, leaving Tommy in the rear. He fancied a change. Tommy saw a Ju 88 slip by in the night. He told Rusty. It hadn't seen them so they let it go. No point in advertising your presence, he thought.

There was much for Norman to marvel over the target. The searchlights were especially impressive – some 60 to a cone – and the flak was particularly heavy, the shell splinters occasionally rattling against the side of the fuselage as a round exploded a little too close for comfort.

The marking was good. Usually, the marking was undertaken by Pathfinders of No 8 Group under Donald Bennett. On this occasion, Sir Ralph Cochrane's No 5 Group had taken the initiative and employed their own techniques based around extremely low-flying Mosquitoes. The bitter arguments and rivalries between the Group Commanders were largely an irrelevance to the men at the coal face. They just wanted the target marked so they could bomb and get the hell out of there. How they marked it, frankly, they didn't care.

The Mosquito 20,000ft below *A Wing and a Prayer* had done its job well, flying through the intense flak and searchlights unscathed. Norman noted numerous fires in the centre of the town and added his cookie and incendiaries to the pyre. He was rewarded with a terrific orange explosion and an obviously successful 'prang'. 'The best yet', as Rusty would later remark.

On the return, they could see far to their starboard side the attack on Karlsruhr. The Germans were in trouble. They didn't have much time to enjoy the spectacle, however, as they were now having troubles of their own. Despite the thick layers of anti-freeze on the wings, severe icing was forming on the port inner mainplane, large chunks were breaking off and hitting the aircraft's body and Rusty's cockpit perspex had been shattered. The airspeed indicator was u/s, as was the 1196 RT aerial (which enabled VHF speech communication between aircraft).

Of bigger concern, however, was the parlous state of their fuel. The situation became more critical still as they exceeded their theoretical maximum endurance but according to Alec's calculations they were still at least 40 minutes from Ludford. They could divert to another station, but nobody liked the idea of arriving at a strange base, in the small hours of the morning, and then the long journey back. It was a quite brilliant piece of airmanship from Curly that got them home, and as the Lancaster tuned off the runway shortly before 07.00 the following morning, the last of the fuel finally expired and the aircraft rolled to a halt. Most likely they had ridden their luck on fumes for the last few minutes of the trip. Curly was the hero of the hour, and deserved the comments of appreciation and gratitude from the others.

The damage caused to the wing by the ice was quite substantial and required a new leading edge. Ted figured this would be good for a couple of days off, but Jock disappointed them all except the Squadron Commander by having the aircraft repaired and ready for operations the next night, Wednesday, for a trip to the Happy Valley.

If their first sortie to Essen had been somewhat benign, the Germans did not afford the RAF the same welcome this time around. They took a long route in through the Ruhr defences and the target was extremely 'hot'. There were contrails over the city, and they saw at least four aircraft shot down. There were no survivors from any of the six Lancaster crews downed that night and only two managed to escape from the single Halifax that became a victim of flak and fighters.

The marking was again excellent. The red and green TIs were clearly visible on the ground, there were plenty of colourful fires and Norman was giving his usual running commentary. For once Rusty was scared. Very scared. He didn't mind admitting. The intense flak, the reports from Ted of German interceptions and the sight of an exploding aircraft right in front of A *Wing and a Prayer* had unsettled him. And he wished to goodness that Norman would shut up.

"Bombs Gone."

Thank Christ for that, Rusty thought. Now for the photograph and they could out of this inferno. But there was a problem. The flare hadn't released.

"Skipper". It was Ted. "The photoflash. It hasn't gone. It's hung up."

"Are you sure?"

'Quite sure skipper I can still see the bloody thing. It's still stuck in the chute."

Rusty thought quickly. "Flight Engineer. Get back and give him a hand, see if you can't force it out."

Curly made his way aft, and was shocked by what he found. When the photoflash was released it was armed by a small propeller which unscrewed as the flash fell and a barometric trigger then fused the device to ignite at a pre-determined altitude. The flash was made safe by a pin which prevented the propeller from turning. When the flash was loaded into the flare chute a wire lanyard was clipped to the pin. The lanyard was long enough to reach the bottom of the chute so that when the flash was released, the pin would not be withdrawn until the flare was clear of the aircraft.

By sheer bad luck the photoflash had dropped down the chute only to stop again just out of arms length. No matter what Ted and Curly did to try and retrieve it, they were unable either to pull it back into the aircraft, or to unhook the lanyard. It would have to stay there – and they would have to pray that it didn't go off. The thought of the flare exploding with a force of more than 200 million candles inside the aircraft was not a pleasant one. Despite the biting cold, both men were now sweating profusely, and Ted reckoned he had aged 10 years. They informed Rusty of the situation.

The journey back was without incident. Rusty's landing approach was even more careful than usual and as the Lancaster's wheels hit the runway with a customary 'bump' the photoflash finally decided to come loose, falling the last few inches out of the tube and onto the tarmac. They waited for the explosion that must surely come but nothing happened. The flare rolled harmlessly to the side.

They had had a lucky escape.

There was some concern at interrogation. No photograph. No raid. At least not one that officially counted towards your '30'. The crew was lucky again. The light of the fires had been sufficient that the Intelligence Officers were satisfied Norman had bombed the target, and there was relief all round. This was somewhat tempered by the news that Pilot Officer Philip Rowe, an extremely popular and equally capable officer was missing with his crew.

As well as Essen, half of the Squadron had also been briefed for Schweinfurt. Rowe had been with the Squadron since October 1943, and was flying his 25th operation. Only the day before he had been recommended for the DFC. Wing Commander Alexander spoke of his 'unconquerable cheerfulness and determination' which, he said, had been 'a source of inspiration not only to his crew, but to the whole squadron.' Since the disaster at Nuremberg the previous month, 101 Squadron had only lost two aircraft, Flight Lieutenant Nimmo on 10th April, and 24-year old Midlander Pilot Officer Ian McDowell on 22nd. This then was a bitter blow. And over the next few days, things were to take a turn for the worse.

Ted was now two-thirds into his tour. Experience had now dramatically increased the crew's chances of survival, although according to official statistics, average losses mounted as crews approached their last half dozen. He put this to the back of his mind.

For his 21st, they went to Friedrichshafen, a town situated on the east shore of Lake Constance where the Zeppelins had once been built. It was now more famed for its factories manufacturing crucial engines and gearboxes for German tanks. Sergeant Carr was deputising for Harry. It was a long trip – more than eight hours – but everyone agreed afterwards it had been worth it. They flew in near daylight conditions, crossing Switzerland and giving Norman the opportunity to marvel at the beauty of Lake Constance shimmering in the bright moonlight. Despite the absence of the Master Bomber's instructions (Rusty couldn't hear anything) Norman had no trouble finding the aiming point, and reported at least three large orange explosions in the target area. He also achieved one of the much sought-after aiming point photographs which were pinned to the noticeboard at base for all to admire.

The raid was indeed a success. The tank gearbox factory was almost completely destroyed and nearly 70% of the town's built-up area was razed to the ground. But there was a cost. Two 101 Squadron aircraft were missing: Flight Lieutenant Dickinson – Deputy 'C' Flight Commander, and Warrant Officer Bertie Noble. Dickinson, and four of his crew would survive as POWs. Noble, who had been twice Mentioned in Despatches, was not so fortunate. Five minutes after leaving the target area, he was intercepted and shot down by Hauptmann Gerhard Friedrich of I./NJG6 (and later its Kommandeur), his aircraft sent into a spin and then exploding in mid-air. Miraculously, two of the crew were thrown clear and survived, only to be interned by the Swiss for their pains. (Friedrich himself would not survive the war. Two months before the war's end, he was killed when the bomb load of a Lancaster he was attacking exploded).

The next day, 28th April, the Squadron was stood down, and the crews slept or spent time at one of their favourite haunts. They had flown three sorties in four days amounting to more than 22 operational hours and were quite literally exhausted. Ted was given a few days well-earned leave which meant he missed Harry's return to duty and a one-third trip to Maintenon in France to blow up one of the Luftwaffe's biggest bomb dumps. Not surprisingly, the explosions seen from 7,000ft in the bright moon were immensely spectacular; Norman dropped his bombs within 800 yards of the target and Rusty had the unusual experience of being able to map read all of the way.

For once, Norman was able to give Alec his pinpoint.

May 3rd was like any other day in Bomber Command's history. But by the end of it, it had proved to be a disaster at least comparable to Leipzig and only eclipsed by Nuremberg the month before. Indeed percentage losses were greater. The only difference perhaps, is that whereas Nuremberg could be seen as The Royal Air Force's equivalent to the Charge of the Light Brigade for its utter futility and pointless waste, the attack on Mailly-Le-Camp was at least in terms of its objectives, a success. Both, however, were a rout that could have been avoided.

Like Nuremberg, no one briefed that day anticipated disaster. The Waughman crew were indeed quite bullish by this stage. The only irritation was that a trip to Northern France would only count as a third. For 30 men of 101, it would be their last.

The airfield was alive with activity. It was a pleasant morning, and the ground crews once again set about their task with meticulous diligence. Each Lancaster at Ludford had been filled with 1750 gallons of aviation fuel, but it was the bomb load that had aroused the most interest and sparked the fiercest debate. Gone were the incendiaries in favour of more heavy explosive: one 4,000lb cookie and 16 x 500lb Medium Capacity bombs suggested a target where destructive power was more important than fire.

At briefing, the Intelligence Officer was similarly meticulous. London, they learned, had been informed via the Resistance that the Germans had assembled a mass of armour and men at an unpronounceable town in the Champagne region of France. It was believed that the depot housed 21st Panzer Divisional HQ, three Panzer Battalions and possibly the remnants of two other battalions withdrawn from the Eastern Front. It also comprised MT buildings and workshops, a tank training ground, firing range, and barrack accommodation for some 5,000 troops. Distasteful so it seems, the timing of the attack was to coincide with the troops' return to barracks at midnight to ensure maximum loss of life. Unusually, they were briefed on three aiming points.

The operation would be a joint effort between No 1 and No 5 Groups. The latter would bomb first, followed by No 1 Group aircraft. 101 Squadron would again be interspersed within the stream to enable a consistent 'layer' of jamming. Aiming point marking was being provided by Mosquitoes of 617 Squadron, the famous Dambusters led by the equally illustrious Wing Commander Leonard Cheshire (who had recently been awarded the Victoria Cross), and the attack was being co-ordinated by Wing Commander Lawrence Deane DSO, DFC, CO of 83 Squadron as Master Controller.

Starting up time came and passed without incident. Rusty taxied *A Wing and a Prayer* from its dispersal to the end of the runway at the head of the long queue comprising 20 Lancasters detailed for that night's attack. Behind him was Lancaster 'R' Roger, piloted by the New Zealander Flight Lieutenant Todd. With final checks completed and a last comment to the crew, ME 565 accelerated to take off speed, Rusty holding the nose down for as long as possible before easing the control column back towards his stomach as the aircraft slowly, impossibly took to the air, clearing the boundary fence and climbing into the moonlit sky. It was 21.50.

Alec gave Rusty the course to steer, South towards Reading then on to Beachy Head. Within a few minutes, Taffy was on intercom. 'Monica , an early-warning radar device against enemy nightfighters was on the blink. Rusty decided to press on. They crossed the Channel, north of Dieppe, climbing to 12,000ft. Ted warmed up his box of tricks, but as yet no 'blips' appeared on his set. Harry, Tommy and Norman tested their guns. Apart from the failure of Monica, the trip was going well. The weather was clear, with good visibility, and the moon was bright. Alec gave Rusty a further course to steer, heading directly, via Compiegne to a pre-designated assembly point some 15 miles north of their target and which was now indicated with yellow TIs. They were late. Rusty reduced height to 7,000ft – their pre-ordained bombing height. Ahead of them, No 5 Group aircraft had started the attack, and there was already a large concentration of fires and explosions in the target area. Their own scheduled bombing time was 00.22. Now they listened for the Master Controller for their turn to bomb.

Ted was now very busy. Blips were appearing with alarming regularity on his screen. It was like Nuremberg all over again. He didn't have to frighten Norman by telling him the night-fighters were on their way because they were already there as they arrived. Unknown to Rusty or any of the other crews in the air that night, they had flown into a trap. Not a deliberate trap, where the Germans had an any prior knowledge of the raid, but rather a trap resulting from delays in the target marking and a breakdown in communication between the marker, the Master Controller and the Main Force.

The cause was a liturgy of poor planning, poor communication and simple bad luck. A badly tuned wireless set within the Master Controller's aircraft meant that his W/T signal for the Main Force to come in and bomb had not been heard. Additional communication from the Deputy Master Controller, Squadron Leader Neville Sparks, was being drowned out by an American Forces radio broadcast and backchat from a handful of the Main Force crews who by now were convinced that the raid was going disastrously wrong.

The effect was further delay and almost inevitably disaster. Confusion meant precious minutes wasted, allowing the

German Controllers to vector their aircraft to the Lancasters' assembly point and the flak gunners to find their range with the resultant mayhem.

"Fighter! Fighter! Corkscrew go!" Ever alert, Harry had shouted the warning.

Rusty threw the aircraft into evasive action on Harry's warning, just as the enemy nightfighter opened fire. Harry and Tommy in the mid-upper turret returned fire, hundreds of rounds of .303 peppering the night sky, the smell of cordite from expended cartridges wafting the length of the fuselage.

"We lost him." There was relief, but no-one relaxed. The assembly point was proving a dangerous place to be, but they had not yet received their orders to bomb.

Harry and Tommy reported several other enemy aircraft in the circuit, watching them intently but holding fire. Rusty could hear some of the crews exhorting the Master Controller to pull his finger out. The language was direct and to the point, but the indiscipline wasn't helping. It made it difficult to hear the instructions from the M/C.

Meanwhile the target was being re-marked. Several slow-burning 250lb incendiaries – known as 'spot fires' – had been dropped, and at last through all the confusion, Rusty received the order he had been waiting for:

"Panthers, come in and bomb Red Spot Fires."

It was 00.24. Pilot Officer Fillingham and Pilot Officer Davidson had heard the same instruction. They didn't need a second bidding. Davidson was the first to bomb. *A Wing and a Prayer* was 60 seconds behind.

Rusty had 190 mph on the clock. Norman was ready. This was not an occasion to hang around. Fighters were everywhere. The night sky was full of fire and colour the like of which Norman had never seen in such splendour. The target a mass of smoke and flame, especially to the East and South East. He aimed for a single Red Spot Fire.

"Bombs Gone."

The mighty cookie and 16 smaller bombs fell away in sequence. Moments elapsed. Rusty held course for the photograph. Tracer rounds from 20mm and 37 mm light flak, lethal at low altitudes, arced in fiery chains past their aircraft.

Then there was a terrific explosion.

For a few seconds the surrounding countryside was bathed in light. Norman could see everything. He could even give Alec a pinpoint if he wanted.

Then an incredible phenomenon.

Norman could see a huge wave rising rapidly towards them – a shock wave – slowly at first and then gathering pace as it rose higher towards their aircraft. This could be dicey, Norman thought. He warned Rusty.

"Skipper, the blast from the explosion has caused a shock wave and it's heading right for us. We could be in for a rough ride."

"OK bomb aimer," Rusty replied. "Let me know when it's likely to hit us."

Norman called the distances, giving Rusty a running commentary.

"4000yds… 3,000…2,000…1000. Brace yourselves!"

Then it struck. The Lancaster was thrown upwards. Rusty kept a loose grip on the controls, flying with the wave rather than against it, all the time in total command. The wave passed through A Wing and a Prayer and further into the sky. It had not been as severe as Norman had feared, but it was still an experience that none of them would like to repeat again in a hurry.

The moment passed. Alec gave Rusty the course to steer, turning right towards Fontainebleau and then on to Chartres.

Behind them, the rest of the Squadron was at last coming in to bomb, the ever steady Flying Officer McKenna in the lead.

But they were not out of it yet. Another fighter flashed by, and a necklace of flak followed them from the target.

Then for the second time that night there was another terrific explosion.

This explosion was directly beneath them, throwing the aircraft quite literally onto its back, hanging in the air for a brief moment and then falling away into a steep power-dive.

Having recovered from the initial shock, Rusty fought for control, heaving back on the control column with all his strength, his feet on the panel in front of him, arms aching with the enormous effort required as the aircraft's speed increased alarmingly. The crew braced themselves. Curly was at Rusty's side now calling out the altitude:

"6,000ft…5,500…5,000…4,500ft…"

Still Rusty pulled at the control column, but the aircraft did not respond. Throttles shut off, anything to recover the dive but still his speed increased until the needle on the Air Speed Indicator edged towards and then beyond 300 mph. The aircraft creaked and groaned, as though any minute its wings might be ripped from its body.

"4,000ft…3,500…3,000…"

Flak was now whistling all around them but Rusty was too pre-occupied to care. He applied violent corrections of rudder and aileron and waited for a response. The aircraft began to answer. The nose slowly and reassuringly began to rise as the dive became less severe.

"2,500ft…2,000…1,500ft …"

At last Rusty, sweating with sheer physical exhaustion, managed to bring A *Wing and a Prayer* onto an even keel as she thundered across the French countryside with its ASI in excess of 360mph, well beyond the aircraft's theoretical maximum diving speed. Rusty caught his breath and looked at Curly with a nod before checking on the rest of the crew:

"Pilot to crew. Check in everybody. Rear Gunner OK?"

"OK Skipper."

"Mid Upper?"

"OK."

"Wireless Operator?"

Silence.

"Wireless Operator? Taffy. Are you OK?"

"Blood! Blood!" came the anguished voice from the bowels of the aircraft.

Rusty turned in his seat and looked back through the Navigator's curtain to see Taffy wiping his face and head. It looked serious.

"Navigator, take a look will you?"

A few seconds elapsed. Rusty was concerned. Alec was laughing.

"He's OK skipper. He's just had a bit of an accident with the pee can, that's all!"

Taffy's 'blood' was in fact urine, spilled from the 'pee' can that the crew used on operations. The 'pee' can was an empty A10 fruit tin, pinched from the Mess, that the crew passed around on long trips when use of the Elsan wasn't practical. It was kept in the warmest spot in the aircraft – the wireless operator's compartment. Rusty's unplanned aerobatics had caused the full can to deposit its load over Taffy, who was now a far from happy man.

With that brief moment of humour over, professional training once more took over. Pilot and Flight Engineer restored the aircraft to 'normal' flying conditions, having first checked for any signs of damage or abnormality in engine performance. Alec worked out their position and gave Rusty a course to steer for home, crossing the coast at Bayeux.

Behind them the last of the Squadron were completing their bombing runs. Pilot Officer Arnold was late on target but lucky to bomb at all, since his bomb aimer – Flight Sergeant Greenaway – had been blinded by a terrific explosion in front of them, possibly even the same explosion that had blown A *Wing and a Prayer* into a dive. The incident was recorded at 00.29.

Last to bomb from the Squadron, and probably the last to bomb that night, was Flight Sergeant J. Davidson flying in 'T' Tommy. He had not heard the M/C calling them to bomb because of interference on the radio set, and because of the back-chat of other pilots. Subsequently his bombing time was recorded at 00.44. By then, A *Wing and a Prayer* was making full speed for England.

A minute later, at 00.45, Squadron Leader Sparkes, the Deputy Master Controller from 83 Squadron who had worked so hard all night to avoid a disaster becoming a catastrophe was picked off by a nightfighter. It was poor reward for such sterling service, although Sparkes and his entire crew would survive.

For some in the Squadron the night was far from over; for others, it had ended almost before it had begun. Flight Sergeant Hingley abandoned his mission over Base, his mid-upper gunner, Sergeant Lewis, having collapsed. Pilot Officer Thomas Drew, a 32-year old married man from Sevenoaks had the inauspicious honour of being almost certainly the first aircraft shot down, succumbing to flak before reaching the Assembly Point. Only one crew member escaped to become a POW.

Pilot Officer King had cleared the target area and was well into the home leg when he was attacked by a marauding Ju88. The Rear Gunner, Flight Sergeant Williams, spotted the aircraft just as it opened fire, 800yds astern. Shells smashed into the rear turret, wounding Williams in the chest and rendering his left arm useless, but not before he had managed to fire off more than 1200 rounds himself and called the pilot to corkscrew. Still Williams kept firing, now joined by his Mid-Upper colleague, Sergeant Bathgate. Between the pair of them, and their pilot, they managed to drive the fighter off, but only after sustaining further damage to the starboard mainplane, flaps and the tail.

Rusty landed at 03.15 after a trip of some five and a quarter hours. Regulations had it that all crews had to be de-briefed before returning to their billets – no matter what state they were in – and Taffy had to suffer many ribald comments and banter from his crew mates and others in the Squadron as to his strange odour. Some gave him a wide berth; others funny looks. Some, who had probably been at the receiving end of Taffy's own brand of humour over the months, couldn't resist a joke or two about his incontinence. Like Curly before him, Taffy was made to suffer.

It had been a mixed night. Everyone agreed that from what they could see of the raid, it appeared as though the target had been completely obliterated. Subsequent reports would indeed confirm that fact, with hundreds of soldiers killed, and large quantities of tanks and motorised transport destroyed. But several crews – including Rusty's – were reporting a number of 'scarecrows' in the target area. A 'scarecrow' was believed to be a special weapon the Germans had devised to cause massive explosions in the sky that looked like an aircraft exploding. Whether myth or reality, at the time they all thought it strange that if the Germans could invent a device to explode with such accuracy, then why couldn't they apparently do the same with their 'ordinary' flak? The force of the 'scarecrow' bursting below A Wing and a Prayer certainly convinced Rusty that what he had seen was indeed an aircraft exploding, and it might have been one of the four Squadron aircraft missing that night.

As well as Thomas Drew, Flight Lieutenant John Keard, Flying Officer George Baker, and Flying Officer Ken Muir were also 'missing'. Flight Lieutenant William Hull DFC, in a 460 Squadron aircraft 'borrowed' by 101 was also overdue. All were in fact dead, and only two of the 39 men missing from the Squadron that night survived.

William Hull was a particularly experienced aircraft Captain, having flown his first operation with 101 in December 1942 and completed his tour in August 1943. During that time he was detailed to carry members of the Photographic Development Unit, and often remained over the target long after discretion might have dictated to allow them to shoot some decent footage.

In terms of losses, it had been a terrible night for Bomber Command. When the final maths had been done, 330 Lancasters had reached the target area, and 42 had been destroyed. Of the airmen who went down with the bombers, 29 managed to evade capture and 21 were taken prisoner. Some 255 were dead.

Rusty noted in his diary: "Ops Mailly Le Camp… What a trip for a third!"

Not long after, as a consequence of Mailly, the 'one-third' order was rescinded. A *Wing and a Prayer* was in a sorry state. The underside had been somewhat 'dented' by the blast, and the paintwork showed considerable sign of scorching from the intense heat of the explosion. Jock and his lads had quite a bit of work to do in patching her up, but by Saturday, the old lady was once again looking her best and ready for operations. An ammunition dump at Aubigne Racan was the target, with take-off in the early hours of Sunday morning, a day before full moon. Indeed conditions were so bright, that they might just as well have gone in daylight, and all got a bit more sleep.

The raid was a complete success, and all nine on board *A Wing and a Prayer* that night were satisfied with the results. Ordinarily, ABC aircraft had a crew of eight, but as a 'seasoned' crew with more than 20 operations under their belts they were carrying a 'Second Dickey' – 21-year old Thomas Allen – to give him the benefit of their experience before being let loose on his own crew. It was a real spectacle. A couple of fighters were seen in the target area but managed to miss them. Marking and bombing were extremely accurate, and the explosion that resulted, Rusty would later note, put Vesuvius in the shade with smoke and flames up to 10,000ft. They bombed at 7,000ft, and almost went up with the target, but Norman got the all-important aiming-point photograph.

'W' wasn't the only aircraft carrying a passenger that evening. Only one Lancaster was lost on the raid, from 576 Squadron, but it carried as its second pilot a No 1 Group Base Commander Air Commodore R. Ivelaw-Chapman. Ivelaw-Chapman had until recently been a staff officer with prior knowledge of the coming invasion. Churchill, no less, ordered that if necessary he was to be assassinated rather than risk betraying the plan. In the event he was captured, but the Germans never realised the significance of the man they had taken.

They landed just before five o'clock that morning, and although warned of a further briefing later that day, were eventually stood down.

The crew was exhausted, but the high jinx continued. Someone had the audacity to steal Ted's precious bicycle. Bikes were a necessary commodity at Ludford to be able to get about the base with the minimum of hassle, and Ted was especially proud of his. The culprit was soon found: Curly had hidden it.

On a fighter affiliation trip, Alec asked Taffy for a QDM – a method of checking their position via wireless transmission.

"Fuck off," Taffy replied.

Not an uncommon rejoinder from Taffy to Alec. Sometimes, Alec suspected, Taffy would give him any old bearing just to keep him quiet, and Rusty knew for certain that Taffy often used the emergency channel when he shouldn't. This time, however, Alec looked round to see Taffy on the floor with his 1154/55 set completely in pieces, attempting to mend a fault.

They flew in a variety of aircraft over the next few days returning to their faithful 'W' on Thursday 11th May for what would prove to be the last time. It was Rusty's 20th and Ted's 24th Operation. It would so nearly be their last.

Hasselt is a small town in Belgium, capital of the province of Limburg. Ted had never heard of it. Nor had any of the others. Its importance, they were informed at briefing, was that it stood at the junction of several important roads and railways from Maaseyck, Maastricht and Liége.

Earlier that day, they had wandered over to the crew room and got their first indication that operations were 'on'. A Battle Order No 510 had been posted, detailing 19 aircraft and their crews. *A Wing and a Prayer* and the name Pilot Officer Waughman was 16th on the list. Flight Lieutenants Knights and Reade were the two senior officers taking part.

Confined to base, several of them rode over to dispersal to see Jock and check on the serviceability of the aircraft. Here they got their first hint at what the target might be. A lowish fuel load – 1,300 gallons against a maximum of 2,154 gallons – suggested a short trip, perhaps Northern France. The bomb load was also revealing. Some 13,000lbs in all, comprising eight 1000lb Medium Capacity (MC) bombs, three American-type General Purpose bombs, and four smaller MC stores. Significantly there were no incendiaries, so a built up area was unlikely.

As had now become routine, the crew kept in regular touch with the 'C' Flight Office. In the early afternoon, a notice appeared informing them that the operational meal was at 18.40 hours, and briefing would follow at 19.30.

Now as the Intelligence Officer continued his talk, they learned that the attack on Hasselt would be a No1 and No 8 Group affair, with 126 aircraft in all, whilst bombers in Nos 3, 5 and 6 Groups were directed against other targets in Belgium and France. The Met Man informed them that the weather en route would be favourable, hazy with patchy cloud that should clear by the time they reached the target.

Pre-take off procedures went off very much as normal. Take-off time – 22.00 – came and went, and Rusty was quickly at the front of the queue, as ever one of the earliest to get under way. The aircraft climbed steadily on track to 12,000ft. There was little to do except keep watch for aircraft – both friendly and hostile – albeit that visibility was no more than 50 yards.

They were in a position 5118N, 46°E, some 10 minutes or 30 to 40 miles from the target when the other aircraft hit them.

Curly had only just had time to let out a cry of alarm. Then he was frantically reaching for the throttle controls, thrusting the levers forward for full power. Something from his training days at St Athan had leaped into his mind that increased power meant more lift. But he didn't really know. It was instinctive. Perhaps it saved their lives.

They had all felt and heard the impact. Harry, who had been rotating his turret at the time, sensed the aircraft shudder and stop in mid-air. Then his shoulders were compressed against the turret and he lapsed into semi-consciousness. Taffy, who was in the astrodome at the time was lifted off his feet. Ted smelled burning rubber, and wished he wasn't sitting on top of the bomb bay. Norman was convinced one of the detonators had exploded, or that the photoflash had been hit by shrapnel and that any moment the bombs would go off.

Rusty had no time for such thoughts. He was struggling to regain control of the aircraft that had quite literally gone limp in his hands, rudder, elevators and ailerons failing to respond to his movements.

Still in command of the situation, Rusty called for the crew to report in. Despite the impact, the aircraft was still flying and Curly's dials indicated the engines and fuel lines appeared undamaged. Then came Norman's turn.

"I'm OK skipper, but my bomb release panel is u/s."

"What about the stores?"

"I'll check." Norman shone the Aldis Lamp into the bomb bay.

"All stores are intact, but there's a large hole in the fuselage and the bomb doors look a bit bent."

"OK. Hydraulics?"

"Hydraulics are OK," answered Curly.

"Let's try opening the bomb doors."

The bomb doors opened successfully. Their options were improving.

"Could we jettison the bombs over the target?" Rusty enquired.

Norman nodded. "Should be able to. My instruments are u/s so I'm not sure how close I can get to the target."

Rusty wasn't especially concerned. They'd come this far they might just as well dump the bombs on the target if they could. Much safer than trying to land with the stores still onboard.

The aircraft was shaking considerably, more than usual, its aerodynamics affected by the buckled fuselage and damage to the tail plane. The noise was also terrific. By now it had become clear that they had been hit by another aircraft, a Lancaster. Harry had seen it fall away into cloud and crash. He reported no parachutes.* The hole in the bomb bay had been caused by the other aircraft's mid-upper turret, probably

---

* There were five Lancasters lost that night. Two from 103 Squadron, based at Elsham Wolds, were accounted for by nightfighters. These were flown by Wing Commander H.R.Goodman AFC, a South African, and Pilot Officer R. Whitley, a victim of Oberleutnant Werner Baake of I/NJG I (one of 41 this Ace and later Geschwader Kommandeur would claim). There were no survivors in either aircraft. The third aircraft was flown by Pilot Officer G.J.R.Clark of 166 Squadron from Kirmington. Three of his crew managed to bail out after similarly being shot down by a nightfighter, Oberleutnant Godfried Hanneck of II/NJG1. The fourth was a 460 Squadron Lancaster piloted by an Australian Pilot Officer J McCleery. He was shot down, crashing in a village 14 miles from Antwerp. Six of his crew survived, while the seventh evaded capture and made it home. Only the fate of the fifth aircraft, a Lancaster of 626 Squadron flown by Pilot Officer C.R.Marriott DFM remains a mystery. According to W.R.Chorley's Bomber Command Losses of the Second World War (1944), Marriott's aircraft 'exploded and fell into the sea djke near Krabbendijke on Zuid Beveland.' Although not conclusive, it seems given the time and location that this was almost certainly the aircraft that struck A Wing and a Prayer, and that Harry saw fall away and crash with a large explosion. Colin Marriott, a 20-year old New Zealander, was despite his age an experienced pilot, recently commissioned, who had previously been awarded a DFM for his actions during a raid on Frankfurt. The remainder of the crew were Sergeant R.S Hollingum, Flight Sergeant J.H Barton (another New Zealander), Sergeant C.R Todd, Sergeant W.A Palmer, and two Canadians, Pilot Officer A.J Muir and Warrant Officer C.W Smith.

killing the gunner instantaneously. Its propellers had torn great chunks out of *A Wing and a Prayer*'s inner engine nacelles, damaging both wheels in the process, but they didn't know that yet. They were still on their bombing run.

The faint voice of the Master of Ceremonies came through the din: "Bomb Flares." Holding the speed at a little over 180mph, Rusty did his best to guide the aircraft through Norman's instructions. Although the main release panel was u/s, the bomb sight itself seemed to be functioning normally and with a number of flares and the railway line in view, Norman called "Bombs Gone", pulling the jettison release as he did so and seeing the bombs explode slightly west of the target near a built-up area.

Ironically they were one of the few aircraft to bomb. Thick haze was obscuring the aiming point and over the course of the next few minutes the MC ordered the bombing to stop.

Norman was happy enough, although in fact he had missed the target by more than four miles! A ropey effort by their normal standards, but thoroughly understandable in the circumstances.

The benefit of targets in Belgium and Northern France was that the time spent over enemy territory was reduced, and the return leg commensurately shorter. But they were all still alert. Their main concern, above keeping the aircraft flying, was nightfighter attack. They were in no condition to take violent evasive action; indeed they were blissfully unaware that the two main longerons, which virtually hold the aircraft together, had been badly cracked near the rear of the aircraft. Any excessive stress could have caused the Lancaster to break up in mid-air. Fortunately Ted reported little activity on the scope. With a damaged rear, Rusty suggested that Harry came up front, just in case the tail end decided to part company with the rest of the aircraft. He refused, preferring to stay in his turret as a look-out. Although now conscious of every creak and moan the aircraft made, and with the bomb doors left open just in case, A *Wing and a Prayer* seemed to be holding herself together well. On leaving the target area they could see, just a little way off in the distance, the attacks taking place at Bourg-Leopold and Louvaine where other 101 Squadron aircraft were involved.

By 01.45 they were only a few miles short of Ludford, identifying themselves to the Flying Controller. On Rusty's instruction, Curly selected the undercarriage release to survey the damage. He shone the Aldis through the bomb bay.

"The port tyre looks OK," Curly reported. "I'll look at the starboard." He peered through the engineer's blister. "The starboard wheel is pretty badly cut," he said. "Looks like you'll have to land on one."

Rusty thought about it for a moment, and then informed the rest of the crew about the situation.

"This could be a bit dicey. If any of you want to bale out…"

His voice tailed away. The crew were already telling him that they didn't fancy that idea and would prefer to take their chances with him.

"Pilot to crew. Crash positions."

Everyone braced themselves for the impact, alone with their thoughts. The gunners preferred to stay in their turrets, and for once Norman chose not stay in the nose for landing.

Rusty kept the port wing slightly down so that the port wheel – the 'good' wheel – would touch first. Skilfully he held the heavy bomber on one wheel, reducing speed gradually before allowing the starboard wheel to drop to the ground. The starboard wheel had indeed been badly damaged, and almost at once the aircraft began to veer dangerously off course. Somehow Rusty managed to keep control of the aircraft as it crashed through the feeder pipes of the FIDO installation by the side of the runway, denting but fortunately not breaking them. It continued hurtling towards the control tower. In the tower, a WAAF of the Flying Control Staff tumbled backwards in fright as she saw the black monster emerge from the dark, screaming towards her at great speed. It was to be the only casualty of the night. At last the bomber came to a halt, looking somewhat ungainly but otherwise unbroken, only a few yards short of the tower. But they were not quite out of danger yet. With a further deft touch, Rusty managed to manoeuvre their battered aeroplane clear of the runway and out of danger to any other returning aircraft.

The relief was palpable. Apart from Curly who had been thrown into the bomb aimer's position on landing, and Harry's earlier concussion, everyone was OK. Taffy summed up their feelings as they clambered out.

"Best landing yet Skipper."

There were a number of repercussions following the events of May 11th. The saddest was the loss of their aircraft. A *Wing and a Prayer* was declared 'Cat AC' and taken off to No 32 Maintenance Unit (MU) to be repaired and rebuilt. Although it would later return to the Squadron under a different letter, it was the last time that Ted, Rusty and the others would fly in her. (She was subsequently lost over the Foret de Cerisy on 9.6.44.) Having shared so much with the aircraft, it was almost like losing one of the crew.

There was happier news, however. The crew's efforts had not gone unnoticed by the Station Commander, Group Captain Patrick King, nor the AOC. The latter ordered (with the AOC-in-C's approval) that Rusty's log book should be endorsed in green ink (red ink was reserved for adverse en-tries) with the following words:

'The pilot, by his flying skill and good airmanship, suc-ceeded in landing his aircraft after a collision on an operational flight with a flat starboard tyre without caus-ing further damage or collapse of the undercarriage.'

And there was more good news later that week at dispersal. The loss of *A Wing and a Prayer* meant they were given a new aircraft, and another 'W' – LL757. Any sadness at the loss of their old war-horse was temporarily lessened, for Rusty and Curly at least, by the fact that their new Lancaster, a B III, was a 'Paddle Steamer'. This meant she had the round-ended propellers, known as Paddle Blades, first used on the Ameri-can-built Merlins and later adopted as standard. Far from being a cosmetic improvement, the blades gave enhanced performance, particularly in the climb.

The question now remained as to what to call their splen-did new beast? They were given their answer the following morning. As they gathered at dispersal, it was immediately apparent that Jock had been busy. Adorning the side of the aircraft was a new piece of nose art, adapted (with appropriate apologies) from a cartoon character within the Glasgow Sunday Post. The illustration depicted a disconsolate figure sitting on an upturned yellow bucket, the contents of which were spilling around his feet. The yellow-haired man was dressed in dark blue dungarees with dull red sleeves and dark brown boots. Underneath him was written the words: 'Oor Wullie.'

That day Rusty took her up for a 45 minute air test and was pleased with the results, but it wasn't until the following Friday (19th) that they got to try her out for real, on an opera-tion to Orleans.

Earlier in the day, Ted had cycled over to dispersal where Rusty was with Jock and the lads. *Oor Wullie* was being fu-elled for the night's operation, and scattered beneath the bomber were the tail fins for the 500lb bombs which had yet to be fitted prior to winching into the bomb bay. Usually they would have been fitted prior to leaving the bomb dump and delivered 'complete', but today for some reason they weren't. Ted disappeared into Jock's hut that he had built to shelter them from the elements and as a useful hide-away for his illicit 'stores'. It was also where Jock hid a radio to 'listen-in' to returning aircraft. Totally against regulations, but in the knowledge that he was out of sight of officialdom, Ted snapped a quick photograph through the open door of *Oor Wullie* with Rusty in the cockpit and Jock on the wing. (It wasn't his first 'sneaky' photo opportunity. Ted had previously 'snapped' Norman on the Elsan, a photograph that now takes pride of place within the official 101 Squadron photo album!).

The operation itself proved to be yet another attack on railway marshalling yards north of the town, and although Norman's bomb sight went u/s, he still managed to hit the target. It was a quiet trip and a 'good prang' – Rusty would later remark – and it gave them just the gentle introduction to *Oor Wullie* that they could have wished. But for the next few trips, Bob Alexander in cahoots with the Squadron Intelligence Officer and the Gunnery Leader needed the Waughman crew for a little experiment.

It was an experiment that could so easily have gone disastrously wrong.

Defensive armament within bomber aircraft had always been a subject worthy of fierce debate. The small calibre Browning .303 machine guns, in whatever quantities, did not have the same range or hitting power as the heavier machine guns and cannon of their nightfighter opponents. The contest was often an unequal one, with cannon shells ripping through an aircraft and its occupants before the gunners had a chance to respond. That's not to say the RAF gunners did not have their fair share of victories, rather that the odds were often heavily stacked against them.

The AOC No 1 Group, Air Vice Marshal Sir Edward Rice, whilst demanding the most from his crews, was also prepared to consider any proposals that could improve his Group's performance and reduce casualties. A chance meeting between Rice and the head of the engineering firm Rose Brothers of Gainsborough led to the design of a new rear-turret carrying two Browning .50 machine guns. Despite the lack of any official interest, Rice went ahead and worked with Alfred Rose with the winning design and the Air Ministry placed an initial production order for the turret in June 1943.

The Rose turret (often referred to as the Rose Rice turret) had several innovative features. 'Standard' hydraulically-operated gun turrets tended to 'over-shoot' when elevating or traversing, requiring delicate adjustments to ensure a perfect alignment between the guns and the target. In the Rose turret, this was eliminated; alignment was always positive to control. The turret was also much roomier, and allowed for two gunners rather than one. The first would aim and fire the guns, while the second would feed target data into the computer-box of the gyro gunsight – in theory at least. In practice, at 101, only a single gunner was employed. A third feature was the cut-away front Perspex. Many gunners had already cut the front Perspex away to provide better vision, but with the Rose turret this aperture was wide enough to serve as a second emergency exit should the need arise.

101 Squadron seemed to be losing a disproportionate amount of aircraft. Many theories have been put forward for this. At the time it was even suspected that the Germans had devised a way of homing in on the ABC transmissions. The

most likely answer is probably far-less technical. It was simply because 101 Squadron flew more operations. Whenever Bomber Command flew, 101 Squadron had to be part of the force. QED the chances of aircraft going missing were greatly increased. Rice decided that 101 Squadron should be the first to be equipped with his new experiment.

Throughout May, Rose turret training got underway. In-between the operations to Hasselt and Orleans, Rusty had taken five gunners, including Harry Nunn and the Squadron Gunnery Leader Flight Lieutenant Hill on one such test, flying ME 517 M$_2$.

DV 302 H-How was similarly equipped, and as the skipper with one of the most experienced crews on the Station, Rusty was asked to test the new rear turret for real. The brief was simple: whereas they weren't being directly ordered to engage the enemy deliberately, they were certainly encouraging Harry to use his new weaponry if at all possible!

After so many recent ops to France and the low countries, it was a surprise at briefing to find their target for tonight – the night of Sunday 21st May – was an old favourite, Duisberg, in the heart of the Happy Valley. Duisberg had long been listed as a 'Primary Industrial Target', its industries being specifically transport, coal and steel. It was also, they were informed, the largest inland port in the world. Incendiaries were once again part of the bomb load, along with the now almost obligatory 4000lb cookie.

The trip out was uneventful, but they experienced 10/10ths cloud virtually all of the way – not what they had been led to expect. It didn't do much for the nerves, scarcely to be able to see one's hand in front of one's face, but they pressed on and reached the target without hindrance from flak. Ted was picking up a few transmissions, but the nightfighters also seemed to be giving them a wide berth. Norman reported several explosions to the South West of the Red TIs marking the target, but other than that there were few of the colourful sights that he usually witnessed – not even a searchlight or two for a bit of variety. Rusty would be spared the usual commentary.

Four and a half hours later they were back at Ludford. Almost immediately they were surrounded with everybody wanting to know whether they'd had a chance to fire the guns. There was almost an air of disappointment from the assembled throng, including the CO, that they had not been attacked and Harry felt that he should somehow have tried harder! He didn't have long to wait, for the very next night they took 'H' again for an attack on Dortmund – again in the Ruhr – and this time there were nightfighters aplenty. Dortmund was as active as Duisberg was moribund. Although there was a slight haze over the target, there was plenty of searchlights and flak to keep Norman happy, and from the moment they crossed the enemy coast Ted was intercepting the first German GCIs.

Harry caught sight of a Ju88 and warned Rusty. So far the enemy hadn't seen them, but he was in range. Now was Harry's chance – a chance to prove the effectiveness of the Rose turret in action. Lining up the fighter in his sights he waited a fraction of a second until he had the perfect shot. Then he squeezed the triggers.

Nothing.

He tried again.

Still nothing.

The grease used to oil the guns had frozen in the extreme temperature, rendering them inoperable. By now the nightfighter had seen them too and moved in to attack. Harry had just enough time to warn Rusty who in turn nipped into a contrail and was lost. It had been a narrow escape.

Harry was pleased to tell them what he thought of their guns when he got back.

Ted was now in sight of home. The ordeal and the uncertainty of knowing whether this trip was the flight where you 'bought it' would very soon be over. He had just three operations to go before the completion of his first tour and comparative safety. That's not to say any of the operations were becoming routine; he was still scared every time he took off. So were the others. Tension was building up amongst the crew even if they didn't realise it. Rusty, going back to camp after an evening out, found himself jumping at the noise of the branches brushing against the side of the bus as it drove too near the curb. It reminded him of the sound of flak splinters crashing against the side of the Lanc.

Having flown two operations in three days there was a slight pause before his 28th and 29th operations, both against the Railway Marshalling yards near the historic City of Aachen. Aachen had two such yards – Aachen-West and Rothe Erde (in the East). Both were vital links in the railway system between Germany and France.

Their specific target on Wednesday May 24th was Aachen-West.

It was an unusually large force (more than 440 bombers) for such a target, with the bomb load comprising a larger number of smaller Medium Capacity and General Purpose bombs.

Just before take-off, Harry realised he had forgotten his beer bottles. Harry, it will be remembered, had taken to throwing the empty bottles out of the rear turret whenever they were over the target, and it had come to be a symbol of good luck. He certainly didn't want to fly without them. Group Captain

King arrived at *Oor Wullie* to find the crew somewhat agitated.

"What's wrong Tiger?" The Group Captain enquired. (He had the remarkable knack of knowing everybody by name – even their nick-names).

Harry explained. Turning to Curly, he told him to hop in the car, at which point with a screeching of rubber and a puff of dust they sped off into the distance. A few minutes later, the Group Captain and Curly returned, brandishing two bottles of beer. Now they could get on with the war.

Rusty took with him another 'Second Dickey' – Pilot Officer Algot Arnell – a novice pilot hoping and expecting to learn how to survive when let loose on his own crew. It meant another crowded cockpit for them all to cope with. Not long after take-off, Alec's Gee navigational aid packed up but with his experience he still had little trouble finding the target. Fighters were once again in abundance and the heavy flak was intense. Their bombing height – 17,000ft – was too high for the light flak to reach them but well within reach of the heavier calibre 88mm and 105mm guns which could be deadly at that range and probably accounted for the 101 Squadron aircraft reported missing, flown by 22-year old Flight Sergeant Wilfred Sullock. (This was the second loss in consecutive operations for 101; Pilot Officer Davidson had gone missing over Dortmund, a victim of flak and fighters, losing five of his crew.)

Despite the very active defences, Norman was easily able to identify his aiming point and dropped his bombs within 400 yards of the target. He was probably one of the closest, for many of the bombs, it was later revealed, landed in the town and the surrounding villages. The net result was that the next night they were sent back to finish the job.

Their second trip to Aachen was similar in many ways. Again they carried a 'Second Dickey' – a 31-year old New Zealand Pilot Officer, Malcolm Steel. And again they carried an identical bomb load. But there were also a number of differences. This time they were briefed on an aiming point East of the town, and not only was the Squadron attacking Aachen but it was also briefed to attack a military base at Bourg Leopold. Their bombing height was also considerably reduced, down to 11,000ft, bringing them into range of the lighter calibre flak. And this time, they didn't miss.

Rusty did a quick descent to the bombing height (as briefed) and held *Oor Wullie* straight and level, his ASI reading a touch above 180mph as he commenced the bombing run. Flak was pretty heavy, with a number of explosions bursting too close for comfort, buffeting the aircraft from side-to-side, the smell of cordite hanging in the air, finding its way under the oxygen masks and into their nostrils. Ted could hear the GCIs clearly calling out their bombing heights as they flew through the defences. He kept it to himself.

Norman was lying prone in his bomb aimer's position, and could not only see the Red TIs, but he also had a visual of the target. Almost at the front of the stream and being one of the earliest to bomb, the aiming point had not yet become obscured by smoke, and as he called 'Bombs Gone" he could clearly see several sticks of 1,000 and 500lb bombs burst around the target indicators. They held on for the photograph, the photoflash igniting below for an image that would show that Norman's bombs overshooting the target by a mere 200 yards.

The devastation was complete. Heavy explosive tore up the railway lines and sidings, and any rolling stock present was completely destroyed. All through-traffic was halted, and Rusty put the nose down, eased the throttles forward and headed for home, away from the flak, a task well-done. Thanks to a spoof raid on Düsseldorf by a small force of six Mosquitoes, the bombers returned relatively unmolested. For Curly, on his last operational sortie, he had little to do to trouble him, except keeping a watchful eye on the dials and gauges, leaving nothing to chance. He had come too far and was too professional to be sloppy now.

Rusty touched down at 04.15, and taxied to their dispersal. He and Curly went through the pre shut-down checks together for the last time as a team, and then the engines, with a final loud crackle, fell silent.

Not all 101 Squadron aircraft had been so lucky that night. One was still outstanding. Nothing had been heard of the crew since take-off, and still nothing would be known as the others turned in for the night after the post-op interrogation. Rusty was particularly saddened, since the missing pilot was Pilot Officer Allen who had been his first 'Second Dickey.' Allen was in fact dead. He had been flying in support of the raid on Bourg Leopold, and their aircraft had been seen to crash on the Sommelsdijk in Zuid-Holland on the island of Overflakkee. There were no survivors.

Whilst the others were happy for him, and not a little envious, Curly found little relief in his new-found freedom. Norman and Ted had both flown 29 operations, and Rusty, Harry, Tommy, Taffy and Alec were only three behind. Curly did not want to break up a successful crew. He wanted to see them all through safely to their '30' – after all, they wouldn't find a better flight engineer on the Squadron or in the whole of Bomber Command! He discussed it with Rusty but officialdom intervened. Curly was summoned to see the MO and told categorically that he was no longer fit to fly. It was nothing to do with nerves, the MO explained, it was simply a physical thing that if he continued to fly he could do himself permanent damage. There would be no argument. He was grounded.

Curly smelled a rat, or at least some form of interference from a higher authority. To his knowledge, no single crew or crew member had come through a tour of operations unscathed since they had joined the Squadron six months before, and this was hard on morale. He sensed, but couldn't prove, that the Group Captain may have had something to do with it.

After a leisurely breakfast, Ted went with Rusty over to the 'C' Flight Office to see whether anything was brewing. The weather was not the best considering the time of year, but there was no doubting that the pace of attacks was on the increase and it was no surprise when Flight Lieutenant McKenna, deputising for the OC 'C' Flight Commander, informed them that operations were indeed 'on' and soon after the Battle Order appeared.

It was now more precisely two months since the massacre at Nuremberg and many new names and faces had appeared on the Squadron. Ted read down the list: P/O Sharp, P/O Holland, P/O Carson, P/O Arnold, P/O Rippon, P/O Corkill, P/O Fillingham, F/L Goeres, P/O Forsyth, F/L Reade, P/O Taylor, W/O Bateman, F/L Wallis, P/O Waughman, Sgt Finlay, P/O Arnell, P/O Davidson, P/O Welsby. He knew scarcely a quarter of them. Certainly he was still cocooned in his own secret world but even amongst the SDO contingent there were few of his friends left.

Time dragged interminably that morning. Ted was always restless and not a little anxious before an operation and was even more so today. By this time tomorrow it could all be over. By this time tomorrow he could be dead. Such was the pressure and the conditions that all aircrew lived with day-to-day. He just wanted it over with.

Briefing came at last. Alexander mounted the platform to reveal the target for tonight. Pray God for a short one, Ted thought. His prayers were answered. The thin strips of coloured ribbon that indicated the route to be taken started at Ludford and ended in France. On the outskirts of Paris by the look of it. More railway yards, no doubt. And they were right. Trappes.

"Another vital rail connection to Nazi Germany…" the Intelligence Officer explained, his voice authoritative, assertive, calm, as though giving a lecture in a school classroom rather than sending men out to destroy or be themselves destroyed.

"You will be a part of a force of 219 Lancasters, Halifaxes and Mosquitoes attacking in two waves…Pathfinder marking will be as follows…Your aiming point will be the East Marshalling Yards …"

The other specialists followed: the Navigation Leader, Bombing Leader, Gunnery Leader. The Flying Controller made sure they could all get away safely and on time, and more importantly, that they could get back. The Met man spoke of difficult weather conditions with the chance of thunderstorms on the way out but that it should be relatively clear over the target.

Alexander closed with his usual valedictory words. Trappes was not the only target that 101 Squadron would be operating against that night. It was also sending up aircraft to protect Lancasters and Halifaxes bombing various coastal batteries and radar stations. It was going to be a busy night.

More time passed. Final briefings were completed. Rusty introduced a spare bod, Flight Sergeant Lees, who would be flying with them as Curly's replacement. They collected their survival packs and filled thermos flasks from the huge urn, then made their way to the Crew Room to change. There was only quiet conversation as Ted pulled on his flying kit.

It was a little after 9-00pm. Day had at last become night and the last vestiges of light were rapidly disappearing. Cloud was heavy, and in a few minutes it would be totally dark outside. The bus arrived to take them to their aircraft. With cumbersome packs and parachute harnesses they clambered on board for the short journey across to dispersal where *Oor Wullie* and Jock would be awaiting. They jumped down. Rusty exchanged a few short words with Jock. Jock knew it would only be a short trip. The fuel load had indicated as much. Fortunately there were no WAAFs around. Previously some of the WAAFs had taken to seeing them off at dispersal, but it made them feel uneasy, as if tempting fate. The crew did not need to be pre-occupied or distracted at a time of such heightened tension. They needed to prepare; to focus. Their women-folk were told – and upset – but duly obliged.

Within the aircraft, Rusty and Flight Sergeant Lees ran through their pre-flight checks and the others did the same. Soon there was nothing left to do except wait. Then start-up time arrived. They assembled around the tail-wheel of the Lancaster to empty their bladders and finish a last, hurried cigarette. Rusty signed the Form 700, handing it back to Jock, confirming *Oor Wullie* was fit for flying. The engines were started and spluttered into life, propellers whirring, staggering at first and then increasing speed until they formed a perfect, almost invisible circle. The new Flight Engineer played with his pumps, dials and switches until he had all four engines synchronised and purring. The chocks were pulled away, Rusty released the brakes and the mighty bomber slowly rolled forward onto the perimeter track, joining the stream of other bombers snaking its way to the take-off position. All around Ludford, the roar of the Merlin engines reverberated, shaking the ground and the huddle of surrounding buildings and makeshift dispersal shacks.

Rusty called each crew member for a final check. Taffy flashed the letter 'W' to the chequered control van with the Aldis and awaited a reply. It came almost immediately. Green. Go. *Oor Wullie* picked up speed quickly. Despite her bomb load of some 13,000lbs of assorted stores, she thundered along the runway until with a gentle bounce and then another she took to the sky and was airborne. Slowly the wheels retracted, and Rusty held her straight and level to increase flying speed before attempting a turn. Alec gave Rusty a course to steer for the Assembly Point. It was just after 22.20.

Oor Wullie gradually made height. Met had certainly been right when they said to expect thundery clouds, but had been disingenuous in predicting their severity. Rusty continued the climb, as the violence of the storm increased. *Oor Wullie* was enveloped by the squall, rain lashing against the glasshouse making it virtually impossible to see outside, not that it would have made much difference. The Lancaster began to climb and then plunge suddenly, as if falling into an enormous black hole or stepping off a cliff. It was a stomach-churning experience which felt like it was turning the aircraft inside out.

There was nothing that Rusty could do except ride it out, and eventually, after several extremely uncomfortable minutes, they at last emerged from the angry clouds into clear skies. They crossed the enemy coast. Ted tuned in his equipment and began scanning for enemy GCI activity. There was little activity on the scope.

"10 minutes to target skipper." It was Alec. Norman made his preparations for the bombing run. The first bursts of heavy flak appeared, but some way off and only spasmodic. The gunners continued to search the night sky, wary of a last moment attack whilst they were at their most vulnerable. Rusty was now flying the Lancaster through Norman's instructions.

Through his headset, Rusty heard the voice of the Master Controller:

"Bomb as instructed."

Norman loaded the height, speed and drift into the computer. He could make out three red Target Indicators on the ground. They were flying at only 8,500ft, there was bright moonlight and the aiming point was clearly visible below them. Rusty had 190mph on the clock.

"Bombs Gone!"

Oor Wullie leapt as the eleven 1000lbs and four 500lbs munitions fell in sequence from the 33ft bomb bay. They held for the photograph, another long 30-seconds, then Rusty dipped the nose and sped out of the target area, pushing the throttles fully forward. Beneath them the first of the bombs exploded across the yards, causing Norman immense satisfaction. It was also his last trip and he had wanted to make it a good one. Several of the bombs had not exploded. They wouldn't. Not for another six days, according to the time delay set by the armourers earlier that day. By then the entire crew would be safe.

Alec plotted the course to steer for home. It was about another two and a half hours flying time. Two and a half hours. A little over 150 minutes and Ted would be safe. Still he scanned the frequencies, jamming what little activity he could detect, Harry and Tommy still ever-alert. Ted's excitement grew, but he didn't let himself become side-tracked. He had come too far now to foul-up at the eleventh hour.

Then the English coast. Soon Rusty was calling the Control Tower for permission to land. Soon after they were in the circuit. As the hour of three o'clock slowly approached, Rusty lowered the undercarriage and flaps, and trimmed the aircraft for landing, reducing speed gradually as the altitude fell away and the doughnut-shaped wheels bit into the runway with a sharp squeal. Throttles now well back and a touch of brake and the aircraft slowed to a taxi, guided back to its dispersal by the faithful groundcrew, anxious to know how the operation had gone and thrilled at the chance of congratulating Ted and Norman on making it through.

Rusty and Sergeant Lees completed their final checks, and the engines were switched off, popping and crackling as they did so in one last exclamation of sound. Then there was silence.

For Ted, the war was over.

Ted's last operation was on Wednesday 31st May. There was little in the way of celebration, merely relief that it was all over. He had taken to marking in his log in the 'remarks' column a tally for each sortie flown. Next to Trappes he wrote '30', and underlined it seven times. His total operational flying time amounted to more than 260 hours: 38.40 day and 221.30 at night. His log was certified correct by Flight Lieutenant McKenna for the O/C 'C' Flight, and ratified by Wing Commander Alexander.

In less than a week the rest of the crew would also complete their operational tours, and the fortunes of the War in Europe would change irrevocably with the D-Day landings.

On Friday 2nd June Rusty and four other Squadron Lancasters went to Trappes again, with a depleted crew. Flight Lieutenant Smith went as Flight Engineer, Flight Sergeant Brookes as Air Bomber and Sergeant Harris as Special Duties Operator. Only Harry, Alec, Taffy and Tommy remained. This time they bombed the other end of the marshalling yards and with a cookie rather than 1000-pounders. It was another successful 'prang' with plenty of fun and games over the target. In the near full-moon conditions, they saw plenty of fighter activity and aircraft going down. Indeed out of the 105 Halifaxes taking part, 15 were lost – a horrendous percentage. But the German didn't have it all their own way. Rusty saw an Me 109 on fire and then explode, and Harry claimed a Ju 88 destroyed – a claim that was later confirmed. It was an outstanding achievement, and a just reward for his hours of patient vigilance guarding their tail.

On the Sunday they flew again to bomb a target at Sangatte, four miles from Calais. On their return they were diverted to Faldingworth where they snatched a couple of hours sleep in the Mess before transport – in the form of the Group Captain – arrived to transfer them back to base. King refused to let Rusty fly on any more operations, no doubt mindful of the major push that was about to commence, and with the others declared his operational tour completed. Only Harry had one more trip to go which he successfully completed the following day, Tuesday 6th June. D-Day.

Whilst the boys were finishing up, Ted enjoyed a few days leave and also attended a board of commission which he easily passed. On 21st June he was posted to 83 OTU in Peplow, Shropshire and then onwards to an Officer Training Centre at the 98 Group Officers School in Lichfield. Commissioned Pilot Officer, he moved to 18 OTU as a gunnery instructor and spent the next few months in relative peace training others to do the shooting. A succession of postings followed until he found himself at Elgin, a satellite of 20 OTU at Lossiemouth when VE Day arrived. Then like thousands of others he was prepared for Tiger Force, the RAF mission to defeat the Japanese which was abandoned after events of the 6th and 9th August with the dropping of the Atomic bombs and Japan's surrender.

With the end of hostilities, certain aircrew such as air gunners and bomb aimers became redundant and were transferred to other duties. Ted was transferred to the Intelligence Branch and posted to the Middle East. At that time, ME Command stretched from Nairobi to Vienna. Ted's first posting was to 700 Air Disarmament Wing in Austria, initially decommissioning German airfields in Southern Austria and later dismantling anti-aircraft installation in Vienna.

After completing a Photo Interpretation course in Egypt, he spent some months with the Desert Air Force in Northern Italy to analyse photo-reconnaissance pictures at the height of Tito's insurgence. He returned to Cairo on airfield security duties at Heliopolis airfield at the end of 1946. Gazetted Flight Lieutenant in July 1946, he then returned to the UK to be demobbed on 8th July 1947 and returned to the Austin Motor Company to complete his apprenticeship.

His life had at last come full circle.

3. POSTSCRIPT

By the end of the Second World War, 101 Squadron had lost 1094 men killed, and 178 Prisoners of War. It was the highest casualty rate of any RAF Squadron during the war.

Happily, all of the Waughman crew survived.

On completing his tour, Rusty was posted to 28 OTU at Ossington, an outfit of Australians who did little to make him feel welcome and believed he was 'swinging the lead' despite having a perforated ulcer! Due for a second tour on Mosquitoes, a surplus of pilots meant he found himself at a Bomber Command Instructors School when the war ended. After a brief spell at Transport Command, Rusty signed on as a regular and held various training appointments, taking part in the Berlin Airlift and latterly being awarded the Air Force Cross to add to his DFC that he had been posted at the end of his tour!. On leaving the RAF, Rusty joined his father-in-law's packaging company from which he finally retired aged 65.

Alec was posted to the OTU in Wymeswold where he instructed on Wellingtons. In November 1944, Wymeswold became a Transport Command Dakota OTU which meant that Alec spent 18 of his remaining years as a 'regular' flying all manner of Transport aircraft from Valettas to Britannias. His final posting before retirement in 1977 was giving navigators low level radar training prior to their further training on Vulcans and Buccaneers. He then spent 10 years as a Civil Servant.

Norman, after a brief rest, returned to fly a tour with 35 Squadron Pathfinders. He completed a further 26 operational sorties and was awarded the DFC. He had always longed for a career in the RAF, and with the war's end finally got his wish. He flew Beaufighters with 45 Squadron in the Far East and Malaya, and Lincolns with 97 Squadron, Bomber Command. He was awarded the Queens Commendation for Valuable Service in the Air in 1952, and an AFC in 1955, the latter for the development of radar bombing. Seconded to the Ministry of Aviation, Royal Radar Establishment in Malvern, Worcs, among the projects he worked on was a High/Low altitude radar navigation reconnaissance system for the ill-fated TSR2. His work was recognised with an MBE in 1966 and the following year he retired from the RAF and pursued a number of business careers until finally retiring to Andorra in 1986.

Curly, awarded the DFM at the end of his tour, was posted to Castle Donnington and then Nutts Corner in Northern Ireland on a flight engineers' course in preparation to fly Avro Yorks. He was next sent to Stoney-Cross to fly freight as far as India, and finally to 511 Squadron at Lyneham to carry passengers to Singapore. He was demobbed in September 1946.

Harry, Taffy and Tommy were posted to training duties, Harry eventually returning to his Canadian Homeland where he played in the wind section for the Nelson BC band, and Taffy returning to the valleys, but only after completing a further tour including the last raid on Hitler's Berchtesgarten retreat. Harry never received any formal recognition for shooting down a German nightfighter, but received the undying thanks of his crew. It was enough. Tommy, the old man of the crew, completed a second tour as a spare bod. Not many gunners achieved this success.

Of their two Squadron Commanders, both also survived.

Wing Commander – later Group Captain George Carey-Foster CMG, DFC, AFC left the RAF in 1946, joining the Foreign Office, establishing the FOs first security department. But for internal politics and power-struggles he may have been able to identify the traitor, Donald Maclean, much earlier, but vital information was not forthcoming and Maclean and Guy Burgess were able to escape. His long career in the Foreign Office was recognised with the CMG, and he retired in 1968. He died on January 14th 1994.

Wing Commander Robert Alexander DFC continued as CO of 101 Squadron until 31st July 1944, but remained close to the Squadron through its official Association. In 1995 he attended the inauguration of the RAF Welford memorial at the crash site of Flight Sergeant Thomas and crew, lost on the Nuremberg raid. He died in January 2000.

John Jossa, the navigator in Paul Zanchi's crew, miraculously survived the war and died in 1990. He never forgave himself for Paul's death.

Rusty's three 'Second Dickeys' were not so lucky. Pilot Officer Thomas Allen was shot down and killed on the night of 27/28th May 1944 on an operation to Bourg Leopold. The young Canadian Pilot Officer Algot Arnell failed to return from an operation to Foret de Cerisy. The third, the 31-year old New Zealand Flying Officer Malcolm Steel perished on Saturday 26th August 1944 near Russelsheim.

Each year, surviving members of The 101 Squadron Association, founded by Dennis Goodliffe, gather at a memorial in Ludford to remember old comrades and village friends. Although their numbers are dwindling, the spirit of the Squadron is still very much alive.

Appendix 1. Ted's Operational Record.

Date	Target	Notes	Sortie	Pilot
24.12.43	Berlin	Abandoned	-	Waughman
29.12.43	Berlin		1	Waughman
2.1.44	Berlin	Abandoned	-	Waughman
5.1.44	Stettin		2	Waughman
14.1.44	Brunswick		3	Waughman
20.1.44	Berlin		4	Sandford
21.1.44	Magdeberg		5	Sandford
27.1.44	Berlin		6	Goeres
29.1.44	Berlin		7	Waughman
30.1.44	Berlin		8	Waughman
5.2.44	Berlin		9	Waughman
9.2.44	Leipzig		10	Waughman
20.2.44	Stuttgart		11	Waughman
24.2.44	Schweinfurt		12	McKenna
13.3.44	Stuttgart		13	Waughman
18.3.44	Frankfurt		14	Waughman
24.3.44	Berlin		15	Alexander
26.3.44	Berlin		16	Waughman
30.3.44	Nuremberg		17	Waughman
20.4.44	Cologne		18	Waughman
22.4.44	Brunswick	Abandoned	-	Waughman
24.4.44	Munich		19	Waughman
26.4.44	Essen		20	Waughman
27.4.44	Friederichshafen		21	Waughman
3.5.44	Mailly-le-camp		22	Waughman
7.5.44	Aubigne-Racan		23	Waughman
11.5.44	Hasselt	Collision	24	Waughman
19.5.44	Orleans		25	Waughman
21.5.44	Duisberg		26	Waughman
22.5.44	Dortmund		27	Waughman
24.5.44	Aachen		28	Waughman
27.5.44	Aachen		29	Waughman
31.5.44	Trappes		30.	Waughman

Appendix 2. The Two 'W's

Lancaster Me 565 – W – A *Wing and a Prayer*.
Avro Lancaster BI.
Damaged in crash landing 11.5.44.
Repaired.
Subsequently lost over the Foret de Cerisy on 9.6.44

Lancaster LL757 – W – *Oor Wullie*
Avro Lancaster BIII
Lost on a raid to Stettin whilst being flown by Flight Lieutenant Stewart on 30.8.44.
The wreckage was recently discovered in Sweden.

Appendix 3. Sources/Acknowledgements

PERSONAL REMINISCENCES, DIARIES, AND LOG-BOOKS OF THE CREW:
Edward 'Ted' Manners
Russell 'Rusty' Waughman
John 'Curly' Ormerod
Alec 'Jumbo' Cowan
Harry 'Tiger' Nunn
Idris 'Taffy' Arndell
Norman 'Babe' Westby.

OFFICIAL RECORDS:
AIR 27/802
AIR 27/803
Form 1180

PUBLISHED REFERENCES:
RAF Bomber Command Losses – 1943 and 1944, W.R.Chorley
Bomber Command War Diaries, Martin Middlebrook
The Nuremberg Raid, Martin Middlebrook
The Bombing of Nuremberg, James Campbell
Bomber Command, Max Hastings
Flying Through Fire, Sean Feast
Bomber Command Handbook, Jonathan Falconer
Night Bombing, Hector Hawton
Aircrew, Bruce Lewis
Bomber Squadron at War, A.J.Brooks
Special Operations, Raymond Alexander
Lancaster at War Vols 1-4, Mike Garbett
Manx Aviation in War and Peace, Gordon Kniverton
Battle Under the Moon, Jack Currie
My thanks once again to Richard Robinson for his thorough research at the Public Records Office.

Photographs

Curly (second left) and ground crew working on the starboard inner Merlin of 'A Wing and a Prayer'.

No 1 Officers Mess at HQ Desert Air Force. Italy August 1946. Ted middle row, fifth from right.

With the Battle of Britain Memorial Flight Lancaster - From left: Alec, Curly, Rusty, Norman and Ted.

Ted's first love: his BSA 500 minus sidecar!

SDO's position - looking forward towards the main spar.

Rusty - showing what he thought of the photographer!

Ted - with a good view of the cockpit blister.

Norman, with finger on the tit. Note the bomb aimer's control panel and release switches.

Bomb aimer's position with Norman and front gun turret.

Curly, Ted and the 'stolen' bicycle

Curly, Rusty and ground crew at dispersal

Ted - with 'borrowed' Irvine.

189

Curly and Ted by rear entry ladder.

Bombing up 'Oor Wullie'.

'A Wing and a Prayer' - with Curly and Norman looking suitably impressed.

191

A very illegal photo. Ted's snapshot of 'Oor Wullie' at dispersal could have landed him in gaol. Note ABC aerials clearly visible.

Newly promoted Pilot Officer Rusty Waughman, aged 20.

Bombs away. Tommy, Norman, Curly and Taffy about to open fire!

*The crew: Norman, Alec, Rusty, Curly, Harry with Tommy (kneeling) and Taffy
(on bicycle). Ted was billeted separately.*

Taffy out in the cold.

Norman, Ted, Curly and Taffy. On snow clearance duty.

Norman, Rusty, Taffy and Curly. Winter. January 1944.

Norman and Taffy frolicking naked in the snow – an image fortunately faded in time!

From Goodbye Berlin. Rusty (centre with flask and fag in mouth) with Norman (fourth right) and Alec (holding glove). The wall map has been deliberately blanked out by the censor.

Food parcels - ready to go.

Crew Room. Waiting for the off…

Mud, Glorious Mud!

By the crew bus. Party of 101 aircrew including Norman (second left with fag).